- colleges and universities must shift emphasis from degree-granting to service to the learner;

- faculty must be redirected through in-service development to use of non-traditional forms and materials;

- educational technology, such as cable television, computers, videotape recordings, and satellite broadcasting, must be used and promoted;

- new agencies must be created to provide and disseminate information, to provide counseling, and to assess and keep student credits.

The Commission directs its recommendations to legislators, foundation members, trustees, planners, administrators, faculty members, and educational association leaders. For these individuals, as well as for adult and continuing education professionals, community college leaders, and all participants in non-traditional programs, *Diversity by Design* is an indispensable document.

JACKET DESIGN BY WILLI BAUM

JOSSEY-BASS PUBLISHERS

615 Montgomery Street, San Francisco 94111
3 Henrietta Street, London WC2E 8LU

LithoUSA573

Commission on
Non-Traditional
Study
Samuel B. Gould, Chairman

DIVERSITY

BY DESIGN

Gift of **SRF** The Sears-Roebuck Foundation

Jossey-Bass Publishers
San Francisco • Washington • London • 1973

The
Jossey-Bass Series
in Higher Education

PREFACE

$\mathbb{N}$ew forms, new structures, new means, and new opportunities for higher education have, in the past two years, become focal points of discussion, planning, and action in the academic world. Accreditation practices are being reexamined, and reappraisal of institutional and student financing is under way. In Great Britain, the Open University has become a highly visible and fully operational entity. In the United States, many new programs and institutions are being designed or are in operation, among them Empire State College of the State University of New York, the University Without Walls, Syracuse University Research Corporation's Five-County Project in New York State, Minnesota Metropolitan State College, and the two new statewide plans being projected by the university and college systems in California.

Meanwhile, the external degree (one which is secured essentially outside the normal framework of resident campus instruction) has moved close to the center of the educational scene. The extension degree, long a characteristic offering of American universities, was supplemented in the 1960s by special degrees for adults. These, in turn, gave rise in the early 1970s to major proposals of an even more unconventional sort. New York State Commissioner of Education Ewald Nyquist announced plans at his inauguration for the Regents External Degree Program, and Carnegie Corporation President Alan Pifer answered affirmatively the question posed by the title of his widely reported speech, "Is It Time for an External Degree?" These external degree programs use many forms of non-traditional education, thus helping to direct both public and professional attention to new approaches to learning.

In 1971, when the Commission on Non-Traditional Study was created, it was one of a few major efforts to assess higher education's response to the pressures of societal change. Today it is one of many such efforts. The Carnegie Commission on Higher Education has sharpened its early general focus and has already published studies and specific recommendations relating to non-traditional study; and more are promised. The Task Force of the Department of Health, Education, and Welfare (better known as the Newman Commission) has issued its thought-provoking report on the role of the federal government in encouraging certain new educational directions. The American Council on Education, the Association of American Colleges, the American Association of Junior and Community Colleges, the Council of Graduate Schools in the United States, the Federation of Regional Accrediting Commissions of Higher Education—these are only some of the national organizations that have formed special bodies to examine and act on the future of higher education with specific emphasis on non-traditional approaches.

Not only has non-traditional study had public and private, organizational and institutional, domestic and foreign encouragement: it has been incorporated into the law of the land. The *Educational Amendments of 1972* to the *Higher Education Act of 1965*, passed by the Ninety-Second Congress, clearly intend to improve postsecondary education by providing assistance to educational institutions and agencies for the following purposes:

(1) Encouraging the reform, innovation, and improvement of postsecondary education, and providing equal educational opportunity for all; (2) the creation of institutions and programs involving new paths to career and pro-

fessional training, and new combinations of academic and experimental learning; (3) the establishment of institutions and programs based on the technology of communications; (4) the carrying out in postsecondary educational institutions of changes in internal structure and operations designed to clarify institutional priorities and purposes; (5) the design and introduction of cost-effective methods of instruction and operation; (6) the introduction of institutional reforms designed to expand individual opportunities for entering and reentering institutions and pursuing programs of study tailored to individual needs; (7) the introduction of reforms in graduate education, in the structure of academic professions, and in the recruitment and retention of faculties; and (8) the creation of new institutions and programs for examining and awarding credentials to individuals, and the introduction of reforms in current educational practices related thereto.*

With the creation of the federal Fund for the Improvement of Postsecondary Education to implement these goals, the direction of the federal government regarding new educational forms seems clear.

As a Commission we are torn between the pleasure of discovering how much interest is now being engendered in adding new options for the learner and the problem of offering in our report more than mere reiteration of what others are already saying. The pleasure far exceeds the problem, however, since it strengthens our original conviction that new educational attitudes and approaches are indeed necessary and in many ways inevitable. There is comfort in discovering that others are sharing our concern and are taking action.

The Commission on Non-Traditional Study was brought into being to examine this whole range of emerging possibilities, to assess their relative significance, and to make recommendations for the future. Taken together, these three parts of the Commission's charge emphasized the need for a broad overview of what is occur-

* Public Law 92–318, June 23, 1972, page 93.

ring educationally today; they emphasized also the Commission's catalytic role in meeting this need and preparing for future needs. The Commission interpreted its task as research combined with action, and it shaped both its work and now this report as a response to that call.

The Commission's program of work consisted of four major elements:

Commission plenary sessions and committee meetings. These meetings, in which the Commission was assisted by members of its own staff and those of ETS and the College Board, deliberated on the concepts underlying non-traditional study and then concentrated on questions of free access to learning, the multiplicity of present and potential educational models and means, the ways student achievement could be recognized and institutional quality assessed, and the ever-present problem of financial implications. A statement of preliminary findings and conclusions from these meetings was issued in a brief pamphlet titled *New Dimensions for the Learner* (Commission on Non-Traditional Study, 1971), and several position papers prepared for these meetings were published under the auspices of the Commission in a book called *Explorations in Non-Traditional Study* (Gould and Cross, 1972).

Hearings and conferences with people representing various agencies and institutions related to higher education. Some of these meetings were specially organized; others were highly informal and individual conversations. A series of six group discussions involved representatives of various sections of postsecondary education: accrediting agencies, private colleges, public colleges and universities, community and junior colleges, alternate systems to traditional education, and educational technology. In addition, a steady stream of visitors to the Commission offices brought many questions and invaluable information. All these sessions were greatly illuminating to the Commission, not only in the knowledge they provided but in the breadth and depth of national interest they indicated.

Commissioned reports and research. Besides the previously mentioned position papers, the most noteworthy among these projects were the following: (1) The commissioning of a book, *The External Degree,* by Cyril O. Houle (1973) with a concluding statement by John Summerskill, a truly important addition to the literature on this subject. (2) Designing and getting support for a major research program in non-traditional education (see Appendix B) undertaken by the Educational Testing Service; the Center for Research and Development in Higher Education at the University of California, Berkeley; The Response Analysis Corporation at Princeton; and the College Entrance Examination Board—a fundamental "survey of the field" which offers a considerable amount of new data not only for enriching this report but for providing background for a series of subsequent reports. (3) Developing from these data and reports a series of interpretive papers by members of the research team for eventual publication. (4) Encouraging the development and support of research on the financial aspects of non-traditional study. (5) Similar encouragement of a study of teaching materials developed by the Open University of Great Britain to determine their applicability to the needs of American students—a study under the auspices of the College Entrance Examination Board, with evaluation of the results to be made by the Educational Testing Service. The Carnegie Corporation of New York and the Educational Foundation of America provided financial support for all these projects.

In commissioning these studies, we tried not to duplicate the work of other institutions, committees, or individuals who had dealt with the subject. As far as possible, the Commission studied their work, and where we found substantial agreement did not try to go over the same ground. A selection of the most important and widely available of these works on modern non-traditional study is in the Bibliography.

Placing the issues relating to non-traditional study before national, regional, and state organizations as well as leaders of individual institutions. The high interest in the Commission's work, as evidenced not only by educational organizations and academic institutions but also by government groups, led to a great deal of participation by Commission and staff members in conferences and meetings of many sorts. The chairman and the executive secretary, to specify just two, have made almost one hundred presentations before such groups, and virtually all the members of the Commission used their various channels of communication to encourage discussion of non-traditional study or associated topics. A large body of reports, plans, analyses, and critiques (some of them negative)' was also stimulated by the Commission's activities or by those of other groups and institutions related to it. And in performing its final catalytic function as a formally constituted group, it called together in late January 1973 people and organizations with ability, influence, and concern, in order to make certain that its recommendations came directly to their attention and to urge action on their part.

This report, therefore, is only one among many efforts of the Commission and should be read with full realization of this context.*

In the Commission's deliberations, two questions arose again and again, the first having to do with semantics, the second with poing of view. Both were basic and both were difficult, even puzzling; in answering them I express what seemed to be the opinions of the Commission members and are certainly my own.

How to define non-traditional study accurately and comprehensively was a stumbling block we never quite hurdled to our satisfaction. The epigram "Tradition is something you make up as you go along" could substitute the word *non-tradition* and be just as meaningful. The term *non-traditional* bothered us; at least one Commission member disapproved of it completely, and others found it irritating. Yet we could not hit upon another term. *Unconventional,* for example, posed the same difficulties as *non-traditional.* Anything that suggested we were dealing with forms or means or models or even concepts that were new was also bound to be a misnomer; we were aware from the start that just about everything we were examining was not new at all. If newness existed, it came in the variety and volume of combinations and structure within which these efforts of the past were being placed and, therefore, in the increased options for the individual. *Alternative approaches* seemed vague and unsatisfactory. Nor did we wish *non-traditional* to be an all-inclusive synonym for the purely technological approaches to learning as exemplified by television, computers, cassettes, or other devices. Even if we found the right term, what chance was there that we could define it with a total inclusiveness or precision?

* A complete synopsis of Commission activities is available from the Commission on Non-Traditional Study, c/o College Entrance Examination Board, 888 Seventh Avenue, New York, New York 10019.

Despite our lack of a completely suitable definition, we always seemed to sense the areas of education around which our interests centered. This community of concern was a mysterious light in the darkness, yet not at all mysterious in retrospect. Most of us agreed that non-traditional study is more an attitude than a system and thus can never be defined except tangentially. This attitude puts the student first and the institution second, concentrates more on the former's need than the latter's convenience, encourages diversity of individual opportunity rather than uniform prescription, and deemphasizes time, space, and even course requirements in favor of competence and, where applicable, performance. It has concern for the learner of any age and circumstance, for the degree aspirant as well as the person who finds sufficient reward in enriching life through constant, periodic, or occasional study. This attitude is not new; it is simply more prevalent than it used to be. It can stimulate exciting and high-quality educational progress; it can also, unless great care is taken to protect the freedom it offers, be the unwitting means to a lessening of academic rigor and even to charlatanism.

Some will object to this definition by attitude on the grounds that this concerned attitude has always existed in all of today's institutions. Others will object because it implies a denigration of our traditional educational practices. Virtually all colleges and universities have changed greatly in the past two decades, and some people naturally believe that the pace of change is already far too swift in education, many times to its detriment. But these objections merely point up the difficulty of drawing clear lines between traditional and non-traditional. There need not and should not be a quarrel between the two.

This conclusion takes us to the heart of the second question: must non-traditionalists advocate the elimination of traditional institutions to make way for new ones? The answer, at least as far as the Commission is concerned, is an unqualified *no*. To propose certain reforms and urge swift broadening of educational opportunity is not to break completely with the past but rather to rectify its weaknesses by building on its earlier and present successes.

There is self-delusion on the part of critics who believe the answer lies in wiping the slate clean and starting over again with a

new and more revolutionary approach, whether it be elitist or more
fully democratic. No lasting solution emerges from this view. History attests to the unreality and lack of pragmatism not only in
trying to turn back the clock by ignoring the expectations of the
many but also in believing that a totally new system, capable of
meeting all of society's needs, can suddenly spring forth fully
grown. Educational change cannot be other than evolutionary even
though the process of evolution can and should proceed with far
more speed than heretofore. More non-traditional approaches are
sorely needed, but they will not suddenly supplant all that is traditional. They will augment, fortify, and enhance traditional phi-
losophies and methods; they will often add new perspectives and
horizons to educational opportunity and possibility; sometimes they
will show clearly that traditional forms have a necessary and irre-
placeable role to play. Yet increasingly they will compete with traditional approaches for students and funds.

The new opportunities afforded under the Educational
Amendments of 1972, whereby students supported directly by
federal grants have a freer educational choice among institutions
than they did, will eventually determine where student needs are
best met and which institutions will prosper. Competition among
colleges in getting students is not a new phenomenon; it has always
ebbed and flowed according to falling or rising student populations
and according to economic conditions. The impact of this competition in the years immediately ahead is hard to predict. It seems safe
to say, however, that while very strong traditional institutions will
continue to thrive, some weak traditional and even some non-traditional institutions will become so inadequate that there will be
little reason for their continued existence.

Meanwhile, an old member of the educational scene is
emerging as a strong competitor for students—the system of alternate
opportunities for learning offered by business, industry, labor unions,
proprietary institutions, the military, cultural agencies, and the like
—a system that may cause a very serious drain of the pool of potential college students. Already it is serious competition, educationally and economically, and its impact will continue to increase.
Our formal educational system, whether traditional or non-traditional, will have to recognize this competition fairly and dispassion-

ately and come to terms with it. Eventually the older system will learn that these alternate means can provide added strength by performing services it is not (or should not be) prepared to undertake and by creating in students a desire for learning which will lead them to colleges and universities.

Despite the apparent dichotomies between the formal and the non-traditional or alternate systems, we must be careful not to make too many distinctions. Few if any colleges or universities today are totally traditional and few are totally non-traditional. A great stirring is under way, bringing many changes, some important and some trivial. This activity can be found at all levels of higher education in varying degrees and in both public and private sectors. The Commission sensed this fact more than a year ago, and, in studies reported here and later, will demonstrate the nature of these changes.

In essence, the evidence is encouraging. Existing institutions are showing under competition that they can adapt to new circumstances and new needs. There is every reason to encourage and assist them in this process. For example, it would be better, especially in the short run, to help existing colleges and universities grant credits and degrees based on non-traditional approaches than to create new degree-granting institutions for this purpose. This course of action will match stability and experience with experimental forms and offer a combination which is both acceptable and reassuring.

In summary, I am saying that the traditionalist and non-traditionalist are not adversaries; that one cannot supplant or supersede the other; and that they are partners in the single grand enterprise of promoting learning. The rigor and discipline of the traditional approach should commend it to the attention of the non-traditionalist; opportunities for individualistic and independent study, for flexible patterns and new techniques, or for lifelong enrichment are equally worthy of notice by the traditionalist.

This assertion is neither empty rhetoric nor a retreat to consensus; it is a realistic affirmation of the total possibility awaiting the public, who voice their rising educational needs and expectations more clearly every day. If these needs and expectations are to be met, we require more institutions of higher learning, more diversity

among them, more understanding of individual students and more
capacity to guide them, more rapid response to change and more
ability to cope with it, more willingness to put students squarely in
the center of the undergraduate learning process, more money and
better stewardship of it, more enthusiastic and wholehearted commitment to the future.

There are a considerable number of recommendations for
action in *Diversity by Design*. Some are bound to be familiar since
the Commission could not possibly avoid touching on a good deal of
what has been advocated by others during the time it has been de-
liberating. These recommendations support and call public attention
to the validity of certain basic educational premises. Several major
recommendations deserve particular attention because, as I see it,
they call for major decisions and action during the next decade. Although they are discussed later in some detail, I summarize them
here for emphasis:

(1) Lifetime learning—basic, continuing, and recurrent—
has a new appropriateness today and requires a new pattern of
support.

(2) Colleges and universities must shift emphasis from degree-granting to service to the learner, thus countering what has
become a degree-granting obsession.

(3) Faculty understandings and commitments must be reoriented and redirected, particularly through in-service development, so that knowledge and use of non-traditional forms and materials will increase.

(4) An organized effort must be made to promote intelligent
and widespread use of educational technology with special emphasis
on programming for cable television, computers, videotape re-
corders, and possibilities of satellite broadcasting.

(5) New agencies must be created to make possible easy
access to information and develop better ways to disseminate it, to
perform guidance and counseling services, and to be assessors and
repositories of credit for student achievement.

(6) New evaluative tools must be developed to match the
non-traditional arrangements now evolving, so that accreditation
and credentialing will have appropriate measures of quality.

(7) Cooperation and collaboration must be encouraged

among collegiate, community, and alternate educational entities so
that diverse educational programs and structures may come into
being.

Education to match our needs—as individuals and as a
society—this is *everyone's* goal. We should work toward it enthusiastically, with a sense of commitment and with confidence that
there are good and valid ways to achieve it, ways that do not lessen
quality even when they are different from traditional standards.
Many pathways lead to excellence just as to the kingdom of heaven,
and neither the traditionalist nor the non-traditionalist has a monopoly on them. *All* the resources for learning, wherever they may
be found and used, can be helpful in the task; *all* people of goodwill
and probity, in education or elsewhere, can be partners in an enterprise so fundamental to a democratic nation.

If I interpret my Commission colleagues correctly, this is the
position from which we start as we offer suggestions and recommendations. I think it is a sound position, not so revolutionary or dramatic as some people might like, but far more so than many realize.
Support for this position seems a more reasonable possibility today
than ever before. The emergence of the National Institute for Education and of the Fund for the Improvement of Postsecondary
Education through the Educational Amendments of 1972 could
mark the beginning of intensive federal efforts to explore and support such needs. Increased responsiveness in both public and private
sectors is also evident. If the recommendations of this report were
to become part of the mainstream of higher education within the
next ten years, we would all look back on the decade of the seventies
as a time when another of the few truly major changes took place in
education.

Acknowledgements

Acknowledgements are owed to many people whose thoughts
and actions are reflected in this report and all that preceded it.

I am grateful to every Commission member and regret that
our time together has come to an end. The members of the Commission showed remarkable forbearance of a chairman who expected them to meet often as a whole group, in committees, or with

guests gathered together for specialized discussions. They came willingly to many parts of the country for long and arduous sessions. And they were always productive in dealing with the many tasks set before them. I wish this report could reflect in some way the pleasure we found in our association, the give and take of long discussions, the occasional sharp divergence of opinions, and the unfailing good humor with which such divergence clarified issues and resolved debate—in a word, the totally professional atmosphere created by colleagues eager to help with the resolution of what to them was an important set of educational issues.

The Commission office was staffed by a small but congenial group. John Valentine, as executive secretary, undertook in the midst of his other duties to roam the country like a modern Johnny Appleseed, making himself available to an unusually large number of organizations who were eager to know more about non-traditional study. Florence Kiey, as executive assistant, lived with amazing equanimity in the midst of a mounting welter of papers to which she always managed to bring order. Her firm, decisive handling of administrative matters accomplished countless tasks, not least of which was her miraculous reduction of mountains of documents to those which were truly significant to the progress of the study. Jean Aherne and Diane Mowatt played their typewriters like virtuosi and assisted in many other ways, such as handling the logistics of special meetings and conferences. I am everlastingly appreciative of their kindness and loyalty.

William Turnbull, president of the Educational Testing Service (ETS), and his counterpart, Arland Christ-Janer, president of the College Entrance Examination Board (CEEB), together with their executive vice-presidents, Robert Solomon and George Hanford, and later Merritt Ludwig, were generous with their time, and their efforts were valuable. Through their cooperation it was possible to have splendid facilities and services made available and to call on the help of staff members of both organizations, including Jack Arbolino, David Brodsky, K. Patricia Cross, Carol Halstead, Rodney Hartnett, J. Quentin Jones, Ernest Kimmel, Carole Leland, John Mullins, Eldon Park, Kay Sharp, John Summerskill, Frances Thomson, John Valley, Jane Wirsig, and Wesley Walton.

Especially merited thanks go to Jane Wirsig of ETS, who

took responsibility for guiding our publications from their conception to their ultimate issuance as well as handling our relations with the communications media. Similarly, John Valley and Jack Arbolino, the authors of the National University model (summarized in Appendix A), which was a major element in causing the Commission to be formed and which stimulated much discussion within the Commission, served as invaluable liaison between ETS, CEEB, and the Commission. K. Patricia Cross, as co-editor of *Explorations in Non-Traditional Study* (Gould and Cross, 1972)` and as one of the chief designers of the Commission's major research projects, was brilliant and tireless in her contributions.

The extraordinary talents of Cyril O. Houle, professor of education at the University of Chicago and a member of the Commission, made much of the task easier and far more effective than it would have been without him. He took time from his professorial duties for two academic quarters to serve as a senior consultant on the vital research program launched under Commission auspices. During that period he also worked with me in planning and creating this report. The great background of knowledge he brought with him, his ability to make calm, lucid judgments and to express them with charm and grace, and his delightful companionship as a colleague place me far more in his debt than I can adequately express.

The Carnegie Corporation of New York, in providing the basic grants for the work of the Commission, illustrated again its commitment to the education of the future and the high vision its leaders bring to this commitment. We could not have had more independence of action for ourselves and at the same time a clearer indication of how deeply interested the corporation was in the progress of our work. The grant from the Educational Foundation of America added greatly to our possibilities for research.

We are appreciative, too, of others who, because of their number, must go unnamed in these acknowledgements. Among them are the pioneering men and women in adult education, extension, and undergraduate education who have long advocated part-time study and special degrees for out-of-school youth and adults. Floyd B. Fischer (1972) spoke for these leaders in his presidential address to the National University Extension Association, when he said: "The spotlight has zoomed in upon us and the concepts and ideals for which we have struggled so long. In a way, we have been like the awkward daughter of the family who worked hard all her life, but who was never really the pride of the family, never quite able to make the grade. Now suddenly, in a manner of speaking, our concepts and ideals are being avidly courted. We appear to be right in the midst of an era of romance."

The Commission on Non-Traditional Study takes this opportunity to state publicly its appreciation of and affection for champions of non-traditional study such as these. We hope that our work helps further their own and that it will stimulate action and assessment in the years ahead. An infinite amount remains to be done. Most of all, we hope that whatever is devised and tested and used will add to the learning possibilities for more and more of our citizens of all ages and in all circumstances. Through such possibilities they may be able to increase their inner strength and their comprehension of the role each human being can play in a humane world.

Princeton, New Jersey   SAMUEL B. GOULD
March 1973

CONTENTS

COMMISSION ON NON-TRADITIONAL STUDY

SAMUEL B. GOULD—*chairman; chancellor emeritus,*
State University of New York

M. ROBERT ALLEN—*dean, Division of Continuing*
Education, University of Miami

HOWARD R. BOWEN—*chancellor, Claremont*
University Center

MARY I. BUNTING—*assistant to the president for*
special projects, Princeton University

HENRY CHAUNCEY—*president, Interuniversity*
Communications Council, Inc. (EDUCOM)

ARLAND F. CHRIST-JANER*—*president,*
College Entrance Examination Board

FRED C. COLE—*president, Council on
    Library Resources*

JOSEPH P. COSAND—*professor of education,
    Center for Higher Education,
    University of Michigan*

BERTRAM H. DAVIS—*general secretary, American
    Association of University Professors*

WALTER G. DAVIS—*director, Department of
    Education, American Federation of Labor and
    Congress of Industrial Organizations*

FRANK G. DICKEY—*executive director,
    National Commission on Accrediting*

W. TODD FURNISS—*director, Commission on
    Academic Affairs, American Council on Education*

RICHARD C. GILMAN—*president, Occidental College*

CYRIL O. HOULE—*professor of education,
    University of Chicago*

C. ALBERT KOOB—*president, National Catholic
    Educational Association*

ELIZABETH D. KOONTZ—*director, Women's Bureau,
    U. S. Department of Labor*

CHARLES A. LeMAISTRE—*chancellor,
    The University of Texas System*

JOHN W. MACY Jr.—*former president,
    Corporation for Public Broadcasting*

LELAND L. MEDSKER—*Center for Research and
    Development in Higher Education,
    University of California*

JAMES PARTON—*chairman of the executive committee,
Encyclopaedia Britannica Educational Corporation*

JAMES A. PERKINS—*chairman of the board and
chief executive officer, International Council for
Educational Development*

ALICE RIVLIN—*senior fellow, Brookings Institution*

FELIX C. ROBB—*director, Southern Association
of Colleges and Schools*

STEPHEN H. SPURR—*president, University of Texas
at Austin*

WILLIAM W. TURNBULL*—*president,
Educational Testing Service*

CLIFTON R. WHARTON Jr.—*president,
Michigan State University*

JOHN A. VALENTINE, *executive secretary*

FLORENCE G. KIEY, *executive assistant*

* *Ex officio members of the Commission*

DIVERSITY

BY DESIGN

Tradition itself cannot constitute a creative force. It always has a decadent tendency to promote formalization and repetition. What is needed to direct it into creative channels is a fresh energy which repudiates dead forms and prevents living ones from becoming static. In one sense, for a tradition to live it must constantly be destroyed. At the same time, destruction by itself clearly cannot create new cultural forms. There must be some other force which restrains destructive energy and prevents it from reducing all about it to havoc. The dialectical synthesis of tradition and antitradition is the structure of true creativeness.

Kenzo Tange
*Katsura—Tradition and Creation in
Japanese Architecture*

1

ACQUIRING PERSPECTIVES

Education, like every other important entity of society, must be responsive to the world it serves or suffer from the constant danger of becoming static and lifeless. Its responses must be active, innovative, contemporary. And those who design education must do more than merely respond; they must develop initiatives of their own that reflect an awareness of changing necessities.

Yet there must be form and order and accountability in such responses. And there must be a powerful creativity that shapes a system to fit the time and the need, creativity that strengthens the process of change by moving in tandem with it. Such creativity must anticipate the future and act upon its foresight; it must experiment and then react forthrightly to the experience the experiments uncover.

In such a system of education, learning is always energized by interrelationships. To be effective, it can never be a collection of random, unjoined segments of information or skills. Its most important characteristic is the weaving together of both information and skills into a tapestry with a framework of motivation and a design that highlights specific and unmistakable goals.

This interweaving begins in the earliest years of life when curiosity is strongest and goals are simplest. For a person to discover the most fundamental elements that surround human life, and for that person to master the basic skills that enable his interaction with other beings—these are all-important steps in assimilating the rudiments of learning. These steps are necessary not only for their intrinsic value but because they already are indicative of how life is to be lived: through independent initiatives in a changing world and interdependent adaptations to it.

An educational system dedicated to the promulgation of true learning establishes its validity, enhances its strength, and maintains its societal relevance in the same way as does the individual—by action and interaction. But as any system advances in age and becomes comfortable in custom, as it grows in size and complexity, it is sometimes more fascinated with keeping learning in good, measurable, controllable order than with recalling its fundamental goals. Original purposes can become clouded and the vitality behind them can all too often be squandered on peripheral enterprises. The student can become less and less the center of concern, and interrelated ideas that bear on human enrichment come to have decreased value among academic faculties and administrations.

This is what some observers—critics and scholars of education, lay citizens, students, and even faculty and administrators—believe has happened in too many of our colleges and universities. They feel that more attention has been given to the form than to the spirit of learning; that knowledge has been neatly departmentalized, with insufficient integration of ideas to permit them to grow in meaning through association. They also assert that learning has been equated with numbers of courses, years of attendance, and meticulous measurement of progress through rigid grading procedures and that attempts at reforming these conditions have not been carefully conceived but have merely involved the abolition of requirements or the development of such reverse images of customary instruction as survey courses which are broad but not deep, touching on everything but thorough in nothing.

Most serious of all, the paramount reason for attending college seems to have shifted from a desire for learning to other motives that are open to serious question. Even the federal government contributed to this shift when it made higher education an escape hatch from military service. And the country at large has made the college degree a basis for conferring social status and a major qualifier for all sorts of employment and increased earning power.

But as the circumstances surrounding a society change (and we all know how swiftly they are changing today) so does its conception of educational needs. In the early days of the Republic higher education largely imitated systems in the traditional societies with which its citizens were familiar: the British and European patterns that were elitist, carefully prescribed, frequently authoritarian. Yet undercurrents of non-traditionalism always flowed through the American consciousness, nurturing a disposition to match educational realities with national purposes. Periodically these undercurrents have risen to the surface and become visible in the mainstream of our culture.

The present restlessness in higher education is the latest of several broad stirrings in our academic history that illustrate, in Cardinal Newman's words, "true enlargement [through] the action of a formative power." The most dramatic of these, although by no means the only important ones, were the land-grant college movement, which began in 1862, and the more recent development of the junior or community college. Both the land-grant college and the community college represented new recognition of the goal of education for the many. Both were originally specific in their efforts to meet a clearly delineated need, but as they matured they incorporated new attitudes toward higher education, focusing on whom it might benefit rather than on precise and inflexible definitions of institutional mission. This adaptability was to be expected of them, and the most successful are those which have enthusiastically fostered such attitudes. They have made great impact on the future of hundreds of thousands of people and therefore on the nation. It is likely that the present movement toward increasing non-traditional alternatives will do the same.

Many educators are now identifying the learner's needs in the context of enlarged horizons for more people. To fulfill these needs requires the formative power of which Cardinal Newman spoke—a power that establishes the validity of the individual's needs and assures their fulfillment through new concepts or adaptations of program and structure, method and form. But novelty is not enough; all such conceptions or adaptations must be able to withstand close scrutiny of their achievements.

Whether the encouragement of learning is based on old or new concepts is, in most instances, irrelevant. The real tests are whether the concepts meet the needs of the learner and are conducive to high-quality results. These criteria take precedence over all else. Additional options for students need not be interpreted as a relaxing of academic rigor if they are properly conceived, professionally supervised, and appropriately evaluated for their true worth. They can, in their various and diverse forms, be part of the continuing movement that has periodically added vitality to higher education.

Tradition of Non-Tradition

It was not merely the creation of the land-grant college and later the community college which signaled the sense of need for a higher education responsive to the demands of society. Some of the central themes and concepts that guide this report have always been in the minds of visionaries and planners. Only sixteen years after the Pilgrims landed, they created Harvard College, and the most important fact about it, as Frederick Rudolph says, is that it was absolutely necessary. A commonwealth could not be created without "leaders disciplined by knowledge and learning. . . . They could not afford to leave its shaping to whim, fate, accident, indecision, incompetence, or carelessness. In the future the state would need competent rulers, the church would require a learned clergy, and society itself would need the adornment of cultured men" (1962, pp. 5–6). A century and a half later, the Northwest Ordinance of 1787 (which has been called the foundation of almost everything which makes the United States unique) declared that "religion, morality, and knowledge being necessary to good government and the happiness of mankind, schools and the means of education shall be forever encouraged."

The colonial colleges grew up in an aristocratic tradition (though some possibility existed for the aristocracy of merit) and the Northwest Ordinance was a statement of lofty principle rather than a practical goal. But by the 1820s, an egalitarian spirit was at work, first in the effort to make the common school available for everyone and then in proposals for widespread higher education. Only nine colleges were created before the Revolutionary War, but by the beginning of the Civil War 950 more existed, of which some 250 still survive. These colleges were conventional in both intention and subject matter. The old ways had worked well in producing the liberally educated men who had created and won support for the new nation. Why should not their heirs, the common people of the new democracy, have the same kind of training? Such was the prevailing viewpoint during most of the period between the wars, though it was gradually altered by a rising belief in non-traditional learning which would seek new goals by new means.

Not until the South, with its aristocratic educational traditions, left the Union could this new pattern be established by Congress, bringing new curricula and new kinds of students to American higher education through the land-grant college. Soon thereafter the lockstep curriculum was broken by the adoption of the elective system, the German university system was imported, and professional education became much more highly developed than before. This new era of higher education broke the dominant traditions of small-college piety and discipline which had lasted for two-and-a-half centuries and laid the foundation for that new tradition which still dominates.

But today, both inside the vast U.S. higher education establishment of more than twenty-six hundred institutions and in the world outside it, there is a quickened and even urgent sense that the long-sought dream of universal and broadly based educational opportunity is still much too far from accomplishment. Recent years have been marked by a fertile creation of new institutions, inventions, systems, theories, and practices, some put forward modestly but many heralded as panaceas. Questions touching every facet of existing schools and colleges—what is to be taught, to whom, by whom, how, when, where, why, and to what effect—are being asked. Non-traditional answers are coming swiftly into being, often in piecemeal fashion, and even more often in isolation from one another. Some of these innovations are nearer to accomplishment than ever before; some are near extinction or have already been quietly laid to rest. Many are still under discussion, and the heightened interest they have aroused has brought the possibility of educational transformation to the forefront of educational attention.

Full Educational Opportunity

In brief, then, the Commission has based its comments and recommendations on a view of history that gives perspective to past, present, and future efforts in higher education. It has examined the traditional educational systems created in the past by traditional societies. It has observed the pressures being brought to bear on our society and our educational systems in modern times—strong pressures stemming from industrial, technological, democratic, and social developments that are challenging and affecting educational philosophy and practice. It has concluded that such pressures represent a major movement of great promise to a democratic people and their higher education.

These pressures are changing our educational tradition. They are moving us away from elitist education based on plutocracy or meritocracy and toward equalitarianism. They are enlarging the definition of the educational process to include learning activities which have taken place along side of, and usually independent from, our existing formal systems. Most of all, they are encouraging an attitude closely attuned to rapid social changes—an attitude of fostering increasing diversity of educational opportunity for our citizenry, but diversity by design rather than by accident and happenstance.

The Commission has tried to identify the specific changes now in being or in prospect as the result of these pressures. It has weighed their validity on the basis of the concepts underlying them, the structures they require, the educational promise they hold, the dangers they create, and their necessity and feasibility, given present circumstances and future hopes. On this basis, the fundamental recommendation of this report simply restates an old ideal:

1. Full educational opportunity should be realistically available and feasible for all who may benefit from it, whatever their condition of life.

Most of the recommendations in this report *are* addressed to specific groups of people, but not this elemental one. It deserves the attention of all who are concerned with the use of education to heighten the quality of American life.

In stating this aim, the Commission hopes to be interpreted as being neither coercive nor unrealistic. Most Commission members have spent their lives in one or several of the realms of education and realize how futile it would be to expect everyone—including the incompetent, the unmotivated, and the isolated—to be fitted into the patterns of formal education, particularly in institutions of higher learning. But Commission members also know that many more Americans than at present can obtain both enlightenment and material benefit from further study. The Commission believes strongly that non-traditional ways of learning can do much to promote full educational opportunity. Those citizens who are now unchallenged or unserved deserve more choices open to them: new curricula, new teaching methods, individualized approaches to learning, instruction scheduled at convenient times and places, different and subtler ways of measuring and assessing accomplishment, and sometimes new institutions especially designed to aid the educationally deprived and forgotten. Appreciable progress toward the goal of full educational opportunity requires both a variety and an abundance of such non-traditional modes. The two key words are *variety* and *abundance,* and neither can be ignored.

The need for variety is probably obvious. What may be less clear is that these various ways of learning should complement one another. It is not enough to alter the present system of higher education merely by making great use of one or two non-traditional features—whether they be correspondence courses, remote telephone hook-ups, examinations for credit, or external degree arrangements. Many and diverse gaps need to be filled if the average citizen is to have the range of services and options that ensures genuine opportunities for effective learning. In addition, it is necessary to acquaint people with study opportunities as they become available, encourage them to take the plunge, and help them stay with the program they choose. Breakthroughs in counseling may be as much needed as breakthroughs in delivery systems. The need for abundance means simply that these various opportunities must be universally available. It is not enough that most approaches referred to as non-traditional are presently in effect somewhere, just as it is irrelevant that these approaches have in some places been in effect for some time. Opportunities to learn must be at hand for anyone who needs them, wherever he may be. And this need for abundance is being felt by *new* populations of students who should be served as well as those who have been insufficiently served in the past.

Somewhere over the land, sometime over the years, someone from among those we talk about as new students has always found his or her way into the formal educational system and has emerged as human interest copy in the newspapers, appropriately gowned and clutching a diploma at commencement time: the breadwinner with a wife and three children, the courageous grandmother, the veteran home from the wars, the suburban housewife ready for a new career, the black ghetto resident, the ex-convict. These and other pioneers were always news, and they still are. They are newsworthy because each one has been a rarity—an example of how the rigidities of the system could be circumvented or, more probably, of how a few determined individuals could adjust their lives to such a system. So long as such achievements continue to be noteworthy events rather than normal educational occurrences, we can be sure we are offering full opportunity on a far too selective basis. For such students, the test of abundance has not yet been met.

Successful use of non-traditional study also depends on assessing the achievement and capability of people at initial, midpoint, and terminal stages of learning—in flexible, sensitive, and practical ways. Educational institutions and programs must be evaluated in terms of what they actually accomplish—we cannot assume they must be doing something right just because their faculty members and deans happen to share essentially the same viewpoints as the members of accreditation teams who evaluate them. Degrees and degree requirements must be redefined. New methods for making credits more portable and functional and for validating and recording educational progress and status in functional and nonmechanical ways must be developed. Also needed are new approaches to financing postsecondary study. Finally, the success of non-traditional study depends on integrating traditional and non-traditional elements in this diverse design.

Many non-traditional approaches to learning respond to the desire of individuals such as these who seek education without being confined within the space, time, place, course sequence, and credit framework characteristic of most educational institutions. They make available education of the greatest potential benefit to the particular individual. This is not a new concept, but even as an old one it has never been completely accepted; in some institutions it has not even been tolerated.

Most teachers have always known that the essence of education—not to mention the absorbing excitement it possesses—is the growth of the individual learner as he develops his potential. Even in traditionally organized institutions, many teachers—and occasionally administrators as well—have managed with remarkable success to retain personal contacts with students and encourage their singular capabilities. But particularly during the past few decades, as hordes of students crowded into American colleges, the institutional components of learning multiplied in number, grew in size, or became intricately complex. Learners, because there were so many of them, had to be considered in terms of their similarities rather than their differences, their categories rather than their uniqueness as persons, and their group patterns and homogeneities rather than their individual possibilities and motivations.

A system has rules, and as a system grows, its rules are ordinarily followed with increasing rigidity. When they are allowed to relax from time to time, unusual results may ensue which should be cultivated rather than ignored. The example of the young Abraham Flexner in the newly formed Johns Hopkins University is instructive here. He entered in 1884 and, as he later recalled (1960):

> soon realized that the funds at my disposal would not permit me to remain in Baltimore more than two years. I determined, if possible, to get my degree by the close of that

period. I doubled up on classes and enrolled for more than
one class at the same hour, attending lectures and recita-
tions in turn. In the class of English, I decided at the outset
that writing daily or weekly themes would be a waste of
time. I therefore explained to Professor William Hand
Browne that I had already been sending from Louisville
communications to *The Nation*. He asked to see them, and
as a result I was promptly excused from a time-consuming
requirement. Professor Kimball was equally sensible in dealing with physics, for I had studied Ganot's *Physics* under
Eaton at Louisville High School. When I mentioned this
fact to him he gave me offhand an oral examination, and,
the result being satisfactory, I was excused and "passed."
 At the end of the first year I found to my horror
that, as the examination came at the same hour as the
classes, I could not be in two or three places at once. In
those easy-going days one simply went to President Gilman
with one's troubles. . . . When I explained my predica-
ment, he said, "Very well; if you know the subjects, that is
all we require. Take such examinations as you please among
those that conflict, and I will arrange to have you examined
separately in the other subjects." I passed in all, and I succeeded in obtaining my degree in two years. Years later I
remonstrated with President Goodnow on the ground that
the Hopkins had, following bad examples everywhere in
evidence, become too efficiently "organized," and in proof
told the story which I have just recounted. Goodnow did
not—could not—believe me [pp. 34–35].

Here (in embryo, as it were) can be seen certain processes
which are today being hailed as non-traditional: credit by examination, advanced standing, independent study, and recognition of
work experience. The fact that they are now considered non-traditional is a clue to how infrequent they had become during the
intervening half-century.
 But since the end of World War II (and partly because of
the pressures it imposed) and especially during the 1960s, methods
of educational individualization have been developed to counter the

uniformities imposed by these very advances in scale. Among the most important of these techniques are a growing array of increasingly sensitive examinations measuring individual abilities and accomplishments; improved guidance techniques based on these measurements and on new theories of personality and therapy; alternative instructional methods and devices for reaching people not adequately responsive to customary approaches; and, perhaps most significantly, the growth of computerized systems that not only underlie these other developments but also bring together various facts about a person into an increasingly complete synthesis of his or her major traits.

None of these systems of individualization is fully humanistic in the true sense of that word. In none of them does a Flexner meet a Gilman. Yet, as mass enterprises grow in education and elsewhere in our society, it is clear that ways can be found to counter an earlier emphasis on uniformity by developing creative adjustments for the individual. An acceptance of the concept of varied individual need, coupled with encouragement of abundant individual opportunity, is the first major step toward searching for these creative adjustments.

When we speak of opportunity for the individual, we speak out of concern not only for that individual alone but for the quality of life within American society at large. Millions of people among us could obtain both enlightenment and material benefit from further study, yet they fail to do so. Some are even to be found in the most economically and intellectually advantaged parts of society, because present practices of higher education do not interest or challenge creative people. Yet most of those who do not fulfill their potential have had obstacles in their way because of certain group characteristics: they are poor, they are women, they live in the wrong place, they are confined by law, they come from a restricted racial or ethnic background, or they are beyond traditional college age.

A nation that respects individual potential and wishes to assist everyone toward full personal growth cannot help but believe in full educational opportunity. With such a belief, the nation declares the essential validity of individual human dignity. It offers everyone the chance to reach all that is attainable, to take a place in society at the highest level possible by crossing as many thresholds to learning as he or she can. It offers opportunity for the young, the mature, the elderly. Such a society is the culmination of a human struggle that has gone on for centuries in which individual men and women have gradually emerged out of the shadows of caste and class, of slavery, despotism, and deadening controls toward a new hope for themselves. That society is still an unachieved goal, but we are closer to it than ever before.

Full opportunity to learn cannot be limited to the young; it must be for everyone, in any walk of life, for whatever purposes are beneficial. It cannot be reserved to a single period of life; it must be a recurrent opportunity: an opportunity to update a skill, to broaden the possibilities of a career whether old or new, or to add intellectual zest and cultural enrichment throughout life. No longer can it be the single opportunity *of* a lifetime; now it must become the total opportunity *for* a lifetime.

2

BROADENING
OPPORTUNITIES

Statistics are legion on the number and nature of young people who drop out of the formal educational system without completing any coherent program of study. One book issued by the Commission (Houle, 1973) summarizes the results of both census data studies and special research and shows that the number of these formally undereducated people will increase by the end of the century if changes in educational policy are not made. The general conclusions are clear: large numbers of able young people do not finish high school, do not go on to college if they do finish, and do not complete their studies if they do attend college; and despite proportional improvements, the number of people at all three levels is growing rapidly.

For a long time, it was assumed that such conditions were evidence of the survival of the fittest, at least in the American setting, or that there was a normal division between those who could profit from academic study and those who could not. Few informed people hold such views any longer.

For example, data on the tests of General Educational Development (GED), a comprehensive battery of examinations designed to measure the extent to which one has mastered the learning required in a general high school education, suggest that a great hunger for formal learning exists in our society. The number of people taking the GED rose from 39,016 in 1949 to 387,733 in 1971 and continues to increase substantially each year. The average person tested is about twenty-eight years old and has had ten years of formal schooling. He typically makes some special preparation for the GED tests either by himself or in a special class. About 31 percent of the persons examined are judged by their state authorities to have met high school standards and therefore receive high school equivalency diplomas. About 41 percent of those who take the examination plan further study. And more than 90 percent of the institutions of higher learning in this country consider the GED "equivalency certificate" equal to a high school diploma for admissions purposes.* This tangible example not only demonstrates how individuals can acquire knowledge and ability over a period of years in non-traditional ways and thereby win a credential that most people secure by conventional means, but also illustrates the widespread desire among Americans for credentials of their knowledge and ability.

Demand for Continued Education

To learn the full extent of the unsatisfied educational desires of adults and their actual participation in study required more than such examples as this or evidence from previous surveys and studies. In order to base its recommendations on comprehensive and current data, the Commission sponsored its own series of research projects, the first of which, here called its "demand" study, surveyed the educational interests and activities of American adults.** In this

---

* All data on the GED supplied by the GED Testing Service of the American Council on Education.

** Appendix B lists this study, coordinated by the Berkeley, California, office of the Educational Testing Service and conducted by the Response

study a representative sample of the approximately 104 million persons aged eighteen through sixty, exclusive of full-time students, living in private households in the United States was chosen in the summer of 1972. This national probability sample of 3,910 household residents paralleled the larger population not only in terms of sex, age, and race, but also level of formal education, region of the country, and size and nature of community residence. Interviewers left questionnaires at the respondents' homes and picked them up on a return visit. If the residents were unable to complete the questionnaire themselves, the survey representative filled it out for them. Responses on the 2,004 completed questionnaires were then tabulated, weighted to compensate for differences in response rate among various subgroups, and applied to the total population. To provide background for the recommendations in the rest of this chapter, some of the major findings will be summarized here. Other data will be reported where relevant in later chapters.

To find how many people are interested in learning anything at all, they asked: "Is there anything in particular that you'd like to know more about, or would like to learn how to do better?" Of the sample, 76.8 percent, representing 79.8 million people, responded "yes." A widely varied list of forty-eight topics was presented to these "would-be learners," and they were asked to note all the subjects that interested them and to identify the one topic they would most like to study or learn. The forty-eight topics were then clustered by the investigators into eight broad areas—"general education," for example, included basic education, biological sciences, creative writing, English language, great books, humanities, languages, physical sciences, and social sciences. The choices for each area of learning are shown in Table 1.

People have a more or less vague ambition to learn many things (the average person chose 3.6 areas), but the difference in emphasis between their total choices and their first choice reflects in a crude fashion the intensity of their feeling about education in

Analysis Corporation of Princeton, New Jersey, together with the several other studies undertaken by the Commission. It includes the names of their principal investigators and the titles of the as-yet unpublished reports from which the data described in the text are drawn. Forthcoming publications growing out of these studies and written by the various investigators will include full technical details of the projects.

Table 1

<small>AREAS OF LEARNING CHOSEN BY WOULD-BE LEARNERS</small>

Areas of Learning	Total choices		First choice	
	Number (in millions)	Percent	Number (in millions)[a]	Percent
Vocational subjects (excluding agriculture)	62.4	78.2	34.3	43.0
Hobbies and recreation	50.1	62.8	10.7	13.4
General education	38.2	47.9	10.1	12.6
Home and family life	44.7	56.0	9.6	12.0
Personal development	43.3	54.3	5.4	6.8
Public affairs	29.0	36.3	3.6	4.5
Religious studies	12.3	15.4	2.4	3.0
Agriculture	8.7	10.9	2.3	2.9

[a] Because of rounding, choice of a topic other than the forty-eight listed, and no response, the figures reporting first choice do not total 79.8 million.

these areas. Vocational subjects hold first place in both distributions but increase their dominance in the first-choice listing while other areas of learning (most notably, hobbies and recreation, home and family life, and personal development) fall off drastically in desirability.

Respondents also reported whether within the past twelve months they had received or were continuing to receive instruction in the eight subject areas in "evening classes, extension courses, correspondence courses, on-the-job training, private lessons, independent study, TV courses or anything like that," rather than as full-time students. To this question, 30.9 percent, representing 32.1 million people, responded "yes." These men and women—here labeled "learners"—were reporting past and present experiences, unlike the "would-be learners," who were reporting mere desires. These two groups overlap substantially, since education is a habit-forming activity: of the "would-be learners" 38 percent were also actual learners in the past twelve months, while 95 percent of the "learners" were also would-be learners. But the distinction between the two populations should be kept in mind in the following summaries: the "would-be learners" represent 79.8 million people who report an interest in more education; the "learners" represent 32.1 million people actually engaged in education.

The areas of learning actually studied by the "learners" are compared to the first-choice areas of "would-be learners" in Table 2. Because the average learner has studied in 1.5 of the areas, the numbers and percentages of the two groups are not comparable, but the rankings and general distribution among the areas show significant differences between actual and intended study—in particular between the expressed interest of would-be learners in vocational areas and the actual choices of learners in recreational fields and hobbies.

Table 2

AREAS OF LEARNING INDICATED AS THE FIRST CHOICE OF WOULD-BE LEARNERS AND STUDIED BY LEARNERS

Areas of Learning	Would-Be Learners		Learners	
	Number (in millions)	Percent	Number (in millions)	Percent
Vocational subjects (excluding agriculture)	34.3	43.0	11.2	35.0
Hobbies and recreation	10.7	13.4	13.4	41.8
General education	10.1	12.6	8.1	25.2
Home and family life	9.6	12.0	4.3	13.3
Personal development	5.4	6.8	3.7	11.4
Public affairs	3.6	4.5	2.1	6.4
Religious studies	2.4	3.0	4.4	13.8
Agriculture	2.3	2.9	1.1	3.4

Both the learners and the would-be learners were asked about their motivation in wanting to study through a list of twenty motives such as "help get a new job," "get away from the routine of daily living," "be better able to serve my church," and "feel a sense of belonging." The would-be learners identified the motives relevant to their first-choice activity and the learners noted those relevant to the studies on which they had spent the most time during the past twelve months.

Table 3 presents the results organized in eight motivational clusters for both populations. The would-be learners profess much more concern with citizenship, religion and spirituality, social reasons, and family life than do the learners, for whom, as seems natural, the authority of an employer, profession, or other authority weighs more heavily. The skeptic might say that socially acceptable motives are more professed than acted upon, since in other clusters, the two populations report fairly similar motivation.

To discover for the Commission why so many of the would-

Table 3

REASONS GIVEN FOR LEARNING BY WOULD-BE
LEARNERS AND LEARNERS

Reasons	Would-Be Learners		Learners	
	Number (in millions)	Percent	Number (in millions)	Percent
Information and intellectual development	56.4	70.7	22.2	69.1
Job and educational development	41.7	52.3	15.3	47.6
Citizenship	24.9	31.2	5.2	16.2
Desire to be a better parent, husband, or wife	23.9	30.0	6.1	18.9
Social reasons	23.7	29.7	7.1	22.0
Requirements of employer, profession, or authority	19.2	24.1	8.8	27.3
Escape reasons	19.2	24.0	6.9	21.4
Church or spiritual reasons	18.9	23.7	5.3	16.4

be learners did not continue their studies, twenty-four obstacles were listed on the questionnaire along with the statement, "Many things stop people from taking a course of study or learning a skill. Circle *all* those listed below that you feel are important in keeping you from learning what you want to learn." The obstacles are listed by rank in Table 4. The number and percentage of responses clearly demonstrate that to a very large number of American adults, education—however much desired—is still too costly, too rigid in its formal requirements, and too inaccessible at the places and times it is needed. Moreover, several of the reasons (such as 3, 7, 8, 11, 14, and 22) suggest the need for greater information, counseling, and individualized reassurance and reinforcement.

Data on the kinds of credit desired by would-be learners for their first choice activity and by learners for their most time-consuming studies were obtained by asking respondents to check the one response listed which appeared most appropriate. The results are presented in Table 5. To the academic community, the relative insignificance of degrees, particularly for actual learners, will probably be the most striking fact reported there, for fully three-quarters of this group are content with no credit at all or with a certificate which indicates that they have performed the tasks required of them. No convincing evidence is available as to why this is the case. But to the Commission, an equally striking fact is that would-be learners are much more interested in receiving credit than are the learners. For example, only 7.9 percent of the learners (representing about 2.5 million people) are working toward a degree while 16.9 percent of the would-be learners (representing 13.5 million people) would like to do so. Are these would-be students being kept away from academic pursuits chiefly because their life and work are too confining or because the educational opportunities available to them are too traditional? Only sustained experience will indicate whether more flexible degree arrangements will enable the millions of would-be learners represented in this study to obtain the knowledge and skills they seek.

Expanding Access

The Commission strongly believes that the United States should undertake this sustained experience. Even the few items of

Table 4

OBSTACLES TO LEARNING CITED BY WOULD-BE LEARNERS

Obstacles	Number (in millions)	Percent
1. Cost, including tuition and all incidentals	42.3	53.0
2. Not enough time	36.9	46.2
3. Don't want to go to school full-time	28.0	35.1
4. Home responsibilities	25.6	32.1
5. Job responsibilities	22.7	28.4
6. Amount of time required to complete program	16.6	20.8
7. Afraid that I'm too old to begin	13.7	17.2
8. No information about where I can get what I want	13.2	16.5
9. Courses I want aren't scheduled when I can attend	12.5	15.7
10. Strict attendance requirements	11.9	14.9
11. Low grades in the past, not confident of my ability	10.0	12.5
12. Courses I want don't seem to be available	9.6	12.0
13. No child care	8.9	11.2
14. Too much red tape in getting enrolled	8.3	10.4
15. Not enough energy and stamina	7.5	9.4
16. Don't enjoy studying	7.0	8.8
17. No transportation	6.7	8.4
18. No place to study or practice	5.7	7.1
19. Tired of school, tired of classrooms	4.9	6.1
20. Don't meet requirements to begin program	4.6	5.8
21. No way to get credit for a degree	4.2	5.3
22. Don't know what I'd like to learn or why	4.1	5.1
23. Hesitate to seem too ambitious	2.2	2.8
24. Friends or family don't like the idea	2.1	2.6
25. Other	1.8	2.2

Table 5

KINDS OF CREDIT DESIRED BY WOULD-BE
LEARNERS AND LEARNERS

Kinds of Credit	Would-Be Learners		Learners	
	Number (in millions)	Percent[a]	Number (in millions)	Percent[a]
No, doesn't matter, don't care	25.9	32.5	19.5	60.8
Certificate of satis- factory completion	16.6	20.8	4.8	15.1
Credit toward high school diploma	4.1	5.1	1.4	4.3
Credit toward skill cer- tificate or license	16.0	20.0	2.2	6.7
Credit toward a two-year college degree	3.2	4.0	.6	2.0
Credit toward a four-year college degree	6.5	8.1	1.1	3.4
Credit toward an advanced degree	3.8	4.8	.8	2.5
Some other kind of credit	.8	1.0	.5	1.6

[a] Not all respondents answered the question on credit desired, and percents in each case were calculated on the total populations of learners and would-be learners.

data already presented from its study of educational demand suggest that the scope and character of the future educational enterprise must be much different from the present formal-education ladder as it operates during the years of youth. Other data from this study will be introduced later leading to additional recommendations, but enough is already obvious at this point to establish the underpinnings for the Commission's recommendations on access to continued education.

2. Basic, continuing, and recurrent education should be strengthened and made more available than at present to adults of the United States.

Partly as a result of social change and partly because of the new interests and needs which individuals encounter as they grow older, it is necessary to lengthen the learning period so that it encompasses not merely the early years of childhood and youth but the whole span of life. As the Commission's first study has clearly shown, millions of American adults are eager to continue their learning. Both the range of things they want to know and their motives for learning are broad and diversified. And the obstacles to this learning can be overcome.

Late in 1972, the International Commission on the Development of Education, established by UNESCO and composed of seven men prominent in their own countries (headed by Edgar Faure, former Prime Minister and Minister of Education of France), issued its report *Learning to Be.* This document and its later supporting memoranda are certain to have profound worldwide consequences. In identifying major strategies for future educational development, the Faure Commission states as its first recommendation, "We propose lifelong education as the master concept for educational policies in the years to come for both developed and developing countries." The Commission on Non-Traditional Study agrees wholeheartedly.

Our Commission believes that in the United States, because of the desired content of adult learning, most organized forms of adult study should probably be sponsored by institutions other than colleges and universities. The respondents in the demand study seem to agree that this should be the case. Of the would-be learners who would like to study some subject, only 9.8 percent chose a public two-year college or technical institute as the setting; 8.5 percent chose a four-year college or university; and 2.6 percent chose a graduate school. Of the learners who had studied during the previous year, only 5.9 percent chose a public two-year college or technical institute, 5.5 percent chose a four-year college or university, and 2.4 percent chose a graduate school. Among the other institutions chosen by respondents from a list of fifteen (such as a public high school, a program sponsored by an employer, a religious institution or group, and a community or social organization) several were in fact selected more frequently than institutions of higher learning (see Table 11).

Elsewhere, the Commission will make recommendations concerning institutional division of labor in serving adult education needs. Here it is only necessary to suggest that such needs fall into three major and equally important overlapping groups—basic studies, continuing education, and recurrent education. The first two, basic studies and continuing education, are well understood. In basic studies, the adult completes a learning program which is normally undertaken in youth: a firm grounding in some area of knowledge, a basic occupational credential, or an external degree are examples. In continuing education, the already formally educated person uses his disciplined abilities constantly to develop his personal, social, or occupational potential by acquiring new skills and knowledge as well as a heightened sensitivity. He may guide his own education or he may turn to some institution for help. When only a few people had a formal education, the opportunity to continue learning was restricted. Now that a high level of learning is widespread, more and more people can take advantage of their disciplined intelligence to engage in continuing education. Thus the implications for large and highly organized programs have become very great.

In the third form, recurrent education, adults set aside periods in their lives to engage in full-time study. This idea is an ancient one; for example, Plato proposed it for his philosopher kings. Moreover, it has long been institutionalized. More than a hundred years ago, the Danes set up a plan which terminated formal schooling for many of their children at the age of fourteen with the idea that they would go back to the *Volkhochschule* at the age of twenty-one or later to spend a significant amount of time in sustained study.

Recurrent education has already been achieved informally to some degree in the United States by the "in-and-out" student as he exercises his options within the current system of education. Other well-organized examples can also be mentioned. For instance, it has been said, perhaps with some exaggeration, that the armed forces have only two basic activities: direct combat and learning. Certainly advancement in the officers' corps depends on being chosen for and then excelling in the series of schools maintained by each branch of the service. In business and industry, as well as in some government bureaus, employee recruitment and retention plans often emphasize the opportunity for education as a benefit, and some companies will pay the tuition for any subject an employee may wish to learn. Educational benefits, some of them substantial, have been won by unions for their members. And planned sabbaticals or informal arrangements for paid study leave are now characteristic of many academic and scholarly institutions.

The Commission feels that this kind of adult education will expand greatly in the future as more and more adults periodically withdraw from the affairs of life to study intensively some topic about which they want or need to know, such study usually being on a credit-free basis. This midlife education may be related to career, to the various roles of social life, or to the personal need for growth. Whatever the originating impulse, recurrent education seems destined to become a major part of American life. The Commission strongly urges college and university policy-makers and administrators to cooperate in—and, if necessary, provide the leadership for—coordinated planning among all educational institutions for all three types of adult education. The Commission also urges them to accept adult education as integral to the work of their institutions rather than offering it only if it pays for itself or helps support other activities. To organizations of educators of adults, the Commission suggests making a broad canvass of financial resources now available from government and private sources for any kind of adult education in any setting. Such a canvass would be invaluable for counselors and others who work with adults.

More important, however, so far as possible, ways should be found to provide financial help to adult students who need it. Thus to legislators, senior government executives, and leaders of industry and labor, as well as educators, the Commission suggests a unified effort to provide financial support for lifelong learning.

3. Financial support (either scholarships or loans) should be provided to all postsecondary school students on which they may draw according to their educational needs, circumstances of life, and continuing or recurrent interests in improvement.

If this recommendation were to be made a reality, the entire span of years of an individual from completion of secondary school to death would be regarded as a single period of time. Every individual would receive as a right a predetermined number of dollar

credits which he could either use up immediately for college, defer
for later use, or balance out according to his needs for initial and
deferred education.

This general idea of the Commission has been well expressed
by the present Prime Minister of Sweden, Olof Palme, speaking in
1969 as Minister of Education:

> Let us regard . . . the entire education coming
> after school education as a *unit,* organizationally, and from
> the point of view of resources. . . . I think that the best
> way for me to illustrate the question at issue is to assume—
> as a hypothesis, representing an extreme, this I am fully
> aware of—that all postsecondary education is organized on
> a recurring basis, that all people, after completing upper
> secondary education, go out into a job, that after some time
> at work they take another period of education, then return
> to a job again, pass through another period of education
> and so on. . . .
>
> For the individual, recurrent education ought to
> have several advantages. We all have need for variety, what-
> ever our occupation is. The student with educational neuro-
> sis and the person in working life with symptoms of stress
> would both perhaps get to grips with their problems if they
> were given the opportunity of a change of activity for a
> time. Leisure time would be used by many in a more valu-
> able way than now and the individual would have a better
> opportunity to get to know his aptitudes. Absolute individ-
> ual failures would be less common, as everybody would have
> a repeated second chance.
>
> Recurrent education should help us on the way
> toward *equality* in society. The interplay between different
> human activities would result in their being regarded in
> various respects as on an equal footing. The understanding
> between different social groups would increase as people
> had more similar experiences. The relations between the
> generations would improve [Organization. . . , 1969, pp.
> 25–26].

To this concept, broad though it is, one further provision can be added: many individuals will want to undertake more recurrent education than is covered by the basic financial support proposed and than their savings will permit. For them, a supplementary loan fund should be available.

The idea of an unrestricted fund of this sort may seem idealistic, but such an incentive system which rewards initiative whenever and wherever it appears has great practical advantages in building both the national economy and the quality of life it supports. The plan also has the great advantage of providing a linchpin for other systems which reward only a few groups in the population, which provide benefits to people at certain age levels but not at others, which offer variable benefits, and which base their selection of recipients on many different criteria. The United States now has many special systems of financing education which are applicable only to restricted populations. Best known are the benefits provided for veterans, but in addition scholarship plans are conducted by some state governments; the lump-sum payments made at the end of Peace Corps, VISTA, and other ACTION programs serve as reserves which can be used for further education; and national and local foundations operate scholarship programs as do individual institutions of higher learning.

The regulations governing such programs usually express highly traditional ideas. Upper age limits are imposed, continuity of attendance is required, or full-time study is demanded. In the veterans' benefits programs, an individual's total credit is based on length of service but a time limit is put on the years during which this credit is available. Apparently the country wishes to show that it is grateful for the military service of a man or woman—but that its gratitude has strict time limits.

In addition to being restrictive, present arrangements are not adequate to meet the expressed needs of the people. The Commission's study of educational demand found that 53 percent of the adult respondents felt that the chief deterrent to taking a course or learning a skill was cost (including books, learning materials, child care, transportation, tuition). The second deterrent, noted by 46 percent of respondents, was "not enough time," a reason which has financial implications since it suggests that in order to study people

might have to forego income. In addition, the Commission's study
of educational supply found that 34 percent of the 1,178 colleges
and universities studied make no financial aid available to part-time
students.

As yet the United States lags behind those European countries which have enacted comprehensive laws to support adults who
wish to engage in education, usually for their own economic advancement. In the United Kingdom, a special tax is levied on every
industry and the amount collected is allocated by special training
boards based on occupations (such as the Iron and Steel Industry
Training Board, the Knitting, Lace and Net Industry Training
Board, or the Carpet Industry Training Board) to those companies
which put forward the best plans for training. The West German
government deals with "employment promotion" by providing in-
centives to those who seek further training. A 1971 French law
begins with the words "Ongoing occupational training constitutes
a national obligation" and guarantees each working citizen the
right to participate in continuing education, including physical and
mental training against obsolescence, personal improvement for job
promotion, retraining, and cultural development. Employers participate by sponsoring courses, authorizing time off for recurrent
education, and contributing mandatory payments at a rate of 0.8
percent of salaries in 1972 rising to 2 percent in 1976. These funds
will equal $800 million in 1973: 0.5 percent of the French gross
national product.

Some European plans of financial credit go beyond occupational training to include all education. For many years, the United
Kingdom has offered a small number of State Scholarships for full-
time study leading to an honors degree "to men and women over
twenty-five years of age who were unable to take a university course
at the normal age." Much broader conceptions are now being examined in other European countries. On this point, the Faure Commission makes the following observation:

> If we suppose that each citizen has the right to a cer-
> tain "quantity" of education during his lifetime, or if society
> guarantees him a certain number of years of education, he
> receives them by drawing "educational cheques" on "recur-

rent education banks." Each citizen has the right to draw a
certain number of modules from his account—throughout
his life and whenever he wishes. A module will correspond
to a certain amount of knowledge and intellectual and emo-
tion development. Bertrand Schwartz (in *L'Education Permanente en l'An 2000*) has taken up this idea, using the
terms "credit-education" or "credit-training," and proposes
four alternative ways of applying it: (a) equal right to education for all at birth, over a certain number of years; (b)'
equal right for all to continued or later education, whatever
the duration of initial studies; for example, the right to
three years' study after the end of formal studies; (c) right
to education depending on the level of the diploma acquired on leaving school; for example, one year for those
failing to reach university entrance level, two years for those
leaving at first university level; (d) right to education depending on profession, doctors having, say, the right to four
years, engineers to three years, etc. [International Commission . . . , 1972, p. 230].

As a first step in stimulating similar progress in the United
States, the Commission on Non-Traditional Study urges Congress,
state legislatures, foundation boards, and college and university
trustees to revise existing restrictive laws and regulations which
prevent current student-aid programs from having the breadth and
continuity that lifelong education requires. The Commission further
suggests that some national nongovernmental agency with broad
expertise in the financing of higher education determine how our
recommendation regarding financial support to all postsecondary
students should be implemented, particularly in the light of other
proposals for ensuring educational opportunity to the individual and
adequate support for colleges and universities.

*4. Many kinds of program options or diverse and flexible
arrangements for study should be available to each student.*

One of the most accepted and revered traditions of academic
life—that success in college is measured by the number of courses
taken, credit hours earned, and information assimilated—is in the
process of being overturned. Today the feeling grows in many

quarters that regardless of the individual's credits and course of study, what really should be measured is competence, adaptability to change, and, in such cases as career education, performance.

Many arguments support this feeling. To begin with, much information hitherto considered the monopoly of schools and colleges is now acquired from many other sources—the journalism and broadcasting media, books, films, travel, alternate systems of education, and experiences of varied types. This pluralism of information revises sharply the functions of formal educational systems. Second, the pace of change places new emphasis on the mastery of long-term principles that apply regardless of short-run change and on understandings that enable a person to cope with swiftly shifting needs and pressures. Third, and most important, individual competence as demonstrated by an ability to use knowledge no matter how it was acquired is, after all, a major goal and result of being educated in the first place.

The implications of these arguments are clear—for curriculum revision, for testing and evaluation, for flexible electives and a new sense of individual responsibility to match that flexibility, and for new and diverse programs within the educational pattern. To break away from custom is never easy, especially when much of the educational establishment remains unconvinced or at least cautious. Without further evaluation of present experiments, some educators will lack confidence to offer unconventional options to their students or to make competence, adaptability, and performance determining factors in educational recognition and reward. But any approaches that come close to providing what students need must be championed by educators and lay citizens alike and must be assessed until their value has been demonstrated or disproved.

Encouragingly enough, data from the Commission's study on the present supply of non-traditional opportunities indicate that a significant number, though not a majority, of American colleges and universities are trying to accommodate the need for flexibility. Of the 1,185 institutions which responded to a Commission questionnaire sent in April 1972 to 2,670 institutions and their branches, 47 percent reported some program of a non-traditional nature, ranging from off-campus majors and accelerated degree programs to experimental branches and technologically taught programs. By inference, the staff concluded that if all institutions had responded, the total figure would be between 35 and 40 percent. These programs, in other words, are not limited to a few well-known and highly publicized schools.*

The Commission's study reveals that these non-traditional programs are fairly recent in origin. Of the 641 reviewed by the staff of the study, 86 percent had been in existence five years or less and 62 percent were less than three years old. Moreover, these programs are designed for a variety of students. Fifty percent are intended for students the same age as those in conventional programs, but 45 percent serve housewives and working adults either exclusively or in addition to students of the traditional age, 41 percent are oriented to special occupational groups, 30 percent are designed for independent learners of all ages, 26 percent serve the unemployed and economically disadvantaged, 18 percent are offered to people confined or beyond commuting distance, 14 percent serve military personnel, and 5 percent are planned for other groups. And while many of these programs are small—18 percent of them enroll fewer than twenty-five students—at least 6 percent enroll more than a thousand.

The Commission finds these programs encouraging but insufficient. It believes that soon a majority of American colleges and universities should offer adaptive programs of this nature. It agrees with Robert Glaser that our society has retained for too long a selective educational mode while aspiring toward an adaptive one. In his presidential address to the American Educational Research Association in 1972, Glaser noted that "a *selective* mode of education is characterized by minimal variation in the conditions under which individuals are expected to learn. A narrow range of instructional options is provided, and a limited number of ways to succeed are available." In contrast, "an *adaptive* mode of education assumes

---

* Background on this survey, conducted by the Center for Research and Development in Higher Education of the University of California, Berkeley, appears in Appendix C. The 1,185 institutions for which data were tabulated are fairly representative of the total population of American institutions of higher learning so far as categories of institutional level and type of control are concerned. It seemed likely to the staff, however, that they probably include a somewhat higher proportion of innovative colleges and universities than does the total population of such institutions.

that the educational environment can provide for a wide range and variety of instructional methods and opportunities for success. Alternate means of learning are adaptive to and are in some way matched to knowledge about each individual—his background, talents, interests, and the nature of his past performance."

This imperative shift in emphasis from selective to adaptive modes requires additional experimental programs and administrators and planners to create them. It demands counselors who can help students select courses and faculty members who can teach them. Also needed are the educational and psychological investigators—particularly those concerned with learning theory, differential psychology, and psychometrics—to help these administrative staff and faculty members understand the distinctive nature of dissimilar learning styles, the differing ability of individuals to respond to various kinds of educational methods, and the implications of these personality differences for the working of colleges and universities.

5. *The needs of some students for new options should not deny other students the choice of staying within the traditional academic framework.*

The educational needs of some college-age and adult students are served better within traditional structures and by traditional means than in any other way. Such structures and means should therefore be included in the options open to students. For at least the next several years, they may well be the choice of a considerable number of students; they will always be the choice of some.

One seemingly simple question to which the Commission has sought answers concerns the number of students at different age levels and stages of educational development and from different social groups who prefer non-traditional to traditional options. The answers are not so easy, even though the Commission's studies have increased the available information. Adults tend to prefer traditional programs when they return to the academic world because they remember them from earlier experience and are more comfortable with them. Minorities, particularly black students, are fearful that new programs or methods—or, in fact, anything non-traditional— may foist something on them that is inferior because it *is* different; thus some are drawn irresistibly toward the most conventional campus settings and the most traditional courses of study. And many other students of customary college age and background will regularly choose a traditional academic approach because they know its long reputation and even prestige, are temperamentally suited to it, and are comfortable within it. Traditional options should not be denied them.

6. *Academic recognition should be extended to those students who complete or continue training to meet the country's technical manpower needs.*

The rapid development of scientific and technical occupational skills, the steady movement of blacks and other minority groups into the highly skilled labor force, and the increasing complexities of urban living already require several types and periods of education and training, a good deal of which may be worthy of academic recognition. The future will bring even greater occupational mobility for our people, already the most mobile population in the world. We move up and down the occupational and social ladder in ways and with a speed unheard of anywhere else. Almost never does anyone live out of a life in exactly the same status as his or her forebears. People are not carpenters because their fathers were carpenters; not even in the professional sphere is there a binding constraint to follow a family tradition. In some ways, Americans have become a rootless, almost nomadic people. We are thus highly individualistic in our ambitions and independent in our efforts to attain them.

An important aspect of this mobility, more evident today than ever before, is the swift obsolescence of certain occupations and the recurring obsolescence of knowledge and techniques within essential occupations. On the one hand, people are no longer needed for certain kinds of work, or fewer are needed to perform it. On the other, new discoveries and social changes make both the technician and the professional out-of-date relatively soon after their initial education and training. Thus the original need to master an occupation is followed by the need to maintain skills, to advance to new levels of responsibility, and, with increasing frequency, to learn a new vocation.

Colleges and universities, and particularly community colleges, are logical entities to carry out a major portion of the highly important tasks of initial and subsequent training. But other, non-academic institutions, such as technical institutes, business, industry, and social agencies, also have a role to play in devising training programs. The interrelationship of these agencies and institutions for the purpose of extending academic recognition should be thoroughly explored and developed. In Recommendation 35, the Commission suggests one means to this end. But the precise nature of such recognition and the criteria on which it should be based are matters for academic institutions, associations, and accrediting agencies to agree upon rather than for the Commission to prescribe. Discussions of these matters should be intensified through the initiative of the accrediting agencies.

7. *Students of traditional college age should have available to them the same non-traditional opportunities as adult students, including the external degree.*

Many colleges and universities, particularly in the private sector, fear that their enrollments and tuition income will drop significantly if non-traditional options become increasingly popular. Although they recognize the pressures toward diverse options from college-age students, who are restive under campus patterns which have been considered standard for so long, they see added problems for themselves if they try to provide both traditional and non-traditional possibilities. They are particularly concerned over the implications of offering the external degree to college-age youth.

One tempting solution to this problem would be for American external degree programs to follow the lead of the Open University of Great Britain, which—out of political necessity as much as anything else—restricted its enrollments to students twenty-one years of age or older. This restriction carefully made clear that the Open University was designed for adult needs, but it eliminated certain possibilities of competition with established British universities.

The Commission has been unwilling to yield to this temptation, even though to do so would eliminate great areas of impending controversy. It has chosen rather to endorse the path of maximum diversity among educational institutions and agencies combined with maximum interrelationships among them. This path will give students of all ages many variations of opportunity, selectively designed to offer education appropriate to each student's capability, motivation, and circumstances of life.

In making this recommendation the Commission has been influenced by the view, expressed by many proponents of non-traditional study, that questions the ultimate desirability of two kinds of degree—internal and external. This point of view looks more closely at the end results of the academic process in terms of individual achievement than at the structures, techniques, and space and time factors through which the achievement takes place. It contends that the ultimate choice among programs is for the student to make, given proper assessment of capabilities and realistic guidance toward goals. (The Commission returns to this point in Recommendation 28.)

Some non-traditional programs such as the University Without Walls are already being developed for college-age students within existing institutions. Others, such as the Regents' Degree in New York State, represent a more radical departure from the norm through new kinds of assessment and flexibility for students of any age. Both programs focus on individual progress, shaped and paced according to individual capacity. The learner, regardless of age, chooses the methods that seem to hold out to him the greatest promise of beneficial results. It seems to the Commission that this is an appropriate option to offer students of all ages.

Information, Advice, and Counsel

Education that permits many choices and relies on individual responsibility for achieving success flourishes or falters very largely in proportion to the effectiveness of the guidance provided. Every student's initiative needs to be directed and shaped by the counsel of others who, through experience and mature judgment and training, can start and move the student along appropriate educational paths. Many such people already exist and are at work. Some are in our colleges or universities; some are in the welfare field or in other community agencies; some work in highly specialized agencies. Many more are needed.

8. Student guidance and counseling services, in specially

*created centers when necessary and appropriate, should provide
expert advice relevant to both individual need and available resources.*

The creation and publicizing of more counseling centers will
add greatly to the potential effectiveness of the diverse opportunities
previously recommended. Their functions will vary with local needs,
but they will ordinarily include referring would-be learners who
know what they want to the places where they can get it; helping
less confident individuals define their interests and needs; identifying
sources of financial support; offering testing services; developing
group counseling situations; and training counselors for individual
institutions.

Programs of non-traditional study should be reinforced by
preliminary and continuing experiences which help students learn
how to learn and which assist them in building confidence in their
capacity to do so. In the Open University in England, the study
centers fulfill this vital function. Many adults who embark on higher
learning do not know how to proceed; they feel insecure and inadequate about the process, and they need advice and assistance on
aspects of it. Instruction in how to learn, guidance through the
varied processes of study, and the availability of both personal and
instructional advice are important for their success. These efforts
should be made with the basic and ultimate purpose of building
independence, not continuing dependence.

These counseling centers should also collect and have available a considerable amount of information on institutions and
programs. To set up these references and keep them current, some
sort of systematized approach is desirable through a regional or
national agency, though adaptations for local resources would be
required. The public library system, for example, is one logical
agent to plan, originate, and monitor if not maintain such a collection of information, as Recommendation 36 suggests in greater
detail.

Illustrations of such centers go back many years. The counseling centers set up in the late 1940s for war veterans might have
developed into broadly based entities of the sort now recommended
had not the restricted nature of their clientele prevented their doing

so. Presently, a large number of colleges and universities house counseling centers for mature women, some of which are beginning to include men among their clients. But probably because of their location, they tend to frighten off all but upper-middle-class persons and those already familiar with college.

It would be wise, therefore, to use facilities that seem approachable to people of many types. The public library, mentioned earlier as an information center, is probably the best community agency to house, staff, and maintain a full guidance and counseling center. The American Library Association (1972) in a report titled *A Strategy for Public Library Change* sets forth a design for such a possibility. The Commission commends it for further study and recommends the financing of a pilot group of such centers, developed in collaboration with other agencies and institutions, in various parts of the country. It also urges national higher education guidance and counseling organizations to consider new types of preparation necessary for proper staffing of these centers. These national organizations could well be one of the major guarantees of well-designed programs and quality results, and thus a great boon to a host of students, particularly those who have been unserved previously.

The discussion of counseling centers by K. Patricia Cross and J. Quentin Jones (1972) represents well the Commission's views on this topic. As they point out, counseling centers should encourage two-way learning. Their function of helping students is clear, though often difficult to arrange. But students bring information to centers as well as take it away, and staff members must be alert to what they hear, for out of the often inarticulate needs and problems expressed to them can grow pioneering non-traditional forms of service.

9. Information regarding groups in our society now denied full access to education should be collected more systematically and continuously than at present and be widely distributed to policymakers in both public and private sectors within and outside the academic scene so that they may take appropriate action.

Certain groups in our society are denied access to education not because of lack of ability or desire but because of such demographic characteristics as sex, age, social status, ethnic background, and place of residence. At present, the decennial United States Census and its annual sample surveys identify the differential educational attainment of several such groups, and special studies by various government and private agencies occasionally report such differences.

It is time for policymakers, not only in education but in other walks of life, to understand clearly the nature of these differences and how deep they are. The present gaps in opportunity for these people and the complicated nature of valid remedies to close these gaps form one of the country's most difficult problems. But solutions begin with understanding, and understanding begins with acquiring and analyzing information. Up to now there has not been enough of either, and so the problems caused by denial of access remain with us.

Isolated instances illustrate successful effort. They show that something can be done, but they show even more how much remains undone. Getting the facts and doing something about them is a task for many agencies and institutions: for the Department of Health, Education, and Welfare in seeing that the information on these groups is available, for academic institutions which can create appropriate programs for them, and for state, local, and private agencies which serve them in other than educational ways.

10. The survey of clientele for non-traditional study begun under the auspices of the Commission should be continued and expanded.

Some of the data reported in the previous chapter illustrate the effort involved in learning about actual and would-be clientele for non-traditional approaches to education. This significant first study of the Commission emphasized the collection of information about the demand for existing non-traditional programs—data on attendance, characteristics of students, and public attitudes toward non-traditional study. Follow-up studies, first as pilot efforts and then as extensive surveys, should be carried out.

We need to know, on the broadest possible scale, not only who prospective students are and what they want to study and why, but also how much time they can and will put into the effort at what times of day or night, where they live (region and city, suburb, or rural area), the amount and nature of their employment, and even the language they speak. Only then can reasonably accurate estimates be made not only of the magnitude of this demand but also of the characteristics it will gradually assume and the nature and extent of financing it will require.

Agencies such as the Educational Testing Service and the Center for Research and Development in Higher Education at the University of California, Berkeley, both of which assisted the Commission in its research activities, are typical of those needed to carry the survey of student demand beyond its present point. Support for this activity could well come from government and foundation sources.

Uniqueness of the Individual

In concluding this set of recommendations on expanded opportunities, the Commission calls attention again to the conflict between our traditional ideal of the dignity and freedom of the individual and our toleration of bigness for its own sake. As technology has become not just the maker of tools but the shaper of men, man has faded steadily into the mass, becoming more and more a manipulated being, caught in the grip of the mass media, computers, and a huge bureaucratic impersonality.

Even in education, where this diminution should be least expected, the individual has been swept into a great collective system that makes him feel puny and of no account, gathering course hours and credits according to standard patterns that brook few exceptions. And so rebelliousness is being shown in every way possible: in dress, in speech, in life style, in independently created courses of study outside the institution's curriculum, in contempt for elders, and in repudiation of everything traditional. Yet all the individual is seeking is what traditionally has always been deemed desirable and, in fact, necessary: a place in the sun as a person, distinct and unique.

We should have learned by now that the key to education for the future is a sense of individual responsibility in each student for choosing, with guidance when necessary, the type of education which will benefit him or her the most. We have the right, even the obligation, to know what motivates each person to learn and to document this motivation, but we have the duty to find ways to respond to this unique motivation.

We no longer have the privilege of delivering homilies on freedom of opportunity and then doing little to deliver either freedom or opportunity. If we choose to be elitist in our institutions, we had better honestly say so. If we choose to open doors for new student populations of all ages, we had better make sure we have workable plans to do so. The expectations we offer must be clear and attainable; otherwise the established system of higher education will soon find itself disestablished. Non-traditional designs of education have become imperative, in short, because the life patterns of modern men and women have themselves become non-traditional.

3

RESHAPING
INSTITUTIONS

When flexibilities and diversities become part of the means and methods of instruction, as they are now becoming, the structure and governance of academic institutions are bound to change. Some structural alterations have already been deliberately and purposefully implemented. Others are being brought about by the effect of circumstances with no deliberate guidance. Even institutions unwilling to relinquish any of their present patterns are being influenced by happenings around them. It seems clear that the introduction of non-traditional elements, whether new degrees, academic programs, credentialing processes, or techniques of instruction or evaluation, soon makes adaptations in structure and governance inevitable. Some organizational changes, already under way as institutions revise policies and programs, are noted here prior to the Commission's structural and governmental recommendations.

Organizational Alterations

Students are pressing for *more interdisciplinary opportunities,* and these broad, problem-oriented studies in which several disciplines share their resources will link department faculties in new and close relationships. Such collaboration has in the past encountered considerable faculty reluctance, but this need not be a permanent roadblock. It can quickly be reduced if faculty members become absorbed with their colleagues and students in examining interdisciplinary problems that are professionally or intellectually exciting and rewarding and if faculty members discover that their individual careers are not threatened when they involve themselves in interdisciplinary arrangements. In the midst of its highly specialized creativity, society is moving steadily toward interdependence on every front. Education can do no less if its leaders intend to help in shaping that society.

Institutional structure is also being affected by the growing acceptance of *interrupted study*—hitherto considered as evidence of individual failure but now viewed positively for its possible contributions to the total learning process. One public urban university, for example, is having to adjust to the fact that the average stay of its "regular" students is seven years rather than the usual four; and its president foresees this pattern of enrollment as increasingly common in universities of its type. The part-time learner is one type of inter-rupted-study student as is the "cooperative education" student—even though he or she now inhabits more than 225 colleges or universities in this country. Another is the intentional "stop-out" student who leaves for a time to travel, to perform some sort of public service, or to search for other maturing experiences that will give new motivation and meaning to his or her educational plan. If any or all of these students are to be accommodated within the framework of a traditional college or university, that framework must expand and change along with the program patterns within it.

The physical characteristics of any institution will be considerably altered if non-traditional education leads to *altered patterns of residence* or to reduced residence on campus. For the adult student in particular, residence in some fashion is important as a variation from the individual's normal living pattern, as the success of conference centers on many university campuses today testifies. Weekend retreats, summer workshops, live-in conferences at various times throughout the year—these can all promote educational growth. From the institution's point of view, these possibilities can lead to different and increased use of campus living facilities to supplement or sometimes substitute for current traditional uses.

In addition to these impacts of interdisciplinary studies, interrupted study, and changes in residence, institutional structures are being affected by *closer articulation* between early and higher education, together with more meaningful relationships among the major levels within higher education itself. This increased cooperation is stimulated by the movement toward diversity and flexibility. An illustration of such articulation is the External Learning Service, under the aegis of the Central New York Consortium, formed in 1971 by the Policy Institute of the Syracuse University Research Corporation. This fifteen-member consortium of two- and four-year institutions is extending the design of external studies from the college to the secondary level. It seeks to "aid people of all ages and educational levels in the region who want to earn *high school diplomas and college degrees* by demonstrating academic competency derived from experience and flexible studies pursued in whole or part outside existing school and college programs" (Policy Institute . . . , 1972b). Alternative paths to the high school diploma are being devised.

The problem of articulation within higher education itself is sizable, as is illustrated by the community college struggle to gain transferability of credit to other institutions. Ground has been yielded grudgingly, but progress is being made. More and more of work done in community colleges is being assessed and given academic value by senior institutions, and more and more community college students are finding transfer easier. Similarly, the Commission on Accreditation of Service Experiences (CASE), developed by the American Council on Education, has made great strides winning academic credit for military courses, and a current pilot program

of the American Association of Junior and Community Colleges
pointed toward the same goal shows considerable promise. At the
upper end of the higher education spectrum there are increased
signs of desire for articulation. The Panel on Alternate Approaches
to Graduate Education of the Council of Graduate Schools is discovering new interdependencies between graduate and undergraduate studies as it examines non-traditional learning possibilities.
Everywhere the present trend toward new relationships is unmistakable.

Recognition of the presence and importance of *alternate systems* of education is leading to additional collaboration that may
affect institutional structures considerably. Significant educational
efforts carried on by the military, government, business, industry,
labor unions, and proprietary schools of many types are now being
looked on from new points of view by the formal education system.
For the first time some merit is seen in drawing closer to these alternate systems rather than standing aloof from them. A meshing of
interests could well reshape some existing institutions along entirely
new lines.

New kinds of *collaboration* which develop among academic
institutions themselves as the result of non-traditional patterns also
affect their structures. As colleges and universities allow students to
move more freely from campus to campus; as adults find it convenient to take their academic work in various places with the
blessing of some single institution; as such non-traditional resources
as computers, television programs, or off-campus laboratories in
oceanography, ecology, and urban development are sponsored by
several institutions; as the talents of selected faculty members are
shared among institutions—as all such developments occur, colleges
and universities become increasingly interdependent and coordinate
their structures and administrative processes accordingly.

Finally, the *financial consequences* of non-traditional arrangements are also causing reexamination of present structures.
While there is still insufficient evidence to indicate precisely what
the cost implications are for students or for institutions, there is little
doubt that these new arrangements will stimulate change. Collaborative efforts of colleges and universities and new forms of instruction could also mean savings, especially if they are substituted for

rather than added to ongoing traditional programs. Start-up costs
for new programs may be high, particularly if electronic equipment
or other apparatus is called for; creation of special centers or bringing in new personnel may also create extraordinary initial outlays.
In the long run, however, these investments may lead to future
economies.

The great array of non-traditional arrangements and programs the Commission has discovered exposes dramatically the
potential weakness of a fragmented approach to their use. Even a
partial list of such arrangements and programs discloses their wide
variety: consortia of institutions and of academic departments;
special guidance and counseling centers for women, returning
veterans, minority groups, and others; tutorials; external degrees;
credit by examination; independent study; work experience and
public service for credit; cooperative education; study abroad;
computer-assisted, two-way telephone instruction; television, correspondence, radio, and videotape courses; weekend, summer, and
other workshops. The broad structure and governance policies of
an institution introducing academic changes such as these must be
devised so as to assimilate such changes with minimum difficulty,
and they must be meshed into a strategy clear enough for all to see.
Diversity by design occurs effectively only when the institution is
properly organized to direct and control change.

The Commission's feeling that colleges and universities are
headed toward restructuring and new forms of governance was
strengthened by the amount of innovation it uncovered through its
study of the supply of non-traditional opportunities, described in
Chapter Two. On the basis of the 641 programs offered by the
1,185 respondent institutions, the staff estimated that probably
between 1,000 and 1,400 innovative programs were conducted by
American colleges and universities in 1972. These programs are
seldom only marginally unconventional. Seventy percent of them
are unusual in the type of student they enroll; 67 percent have distinctive locations; 57 percent use unconventional instruction methods; and 48 percent focus on unorthodox subject matter or content.
Only 21 percent of the institutions studied are distinguished by a
single non-traditional feature (students, location, method of instruction, or content). Thirty-six percent have two, 24 percent have

three, and 19 percent have all four features. Among the programs
to which institutions are planning to devote most resources in the
future, 51 percent permit students to determine their own pace for
completing work; 33 percent allow students to complete their work
at several different campuses; 28 percent grant students and faculty
the opportunity to establish learning contracts between themselves;
and in another 28 percent, students may begin the program at any
time rather than only at the start of a term.

These programs are appearing in institutions of all types;
and although different types of institutions differ in their openness
to non-traditional concepts, as Table 6 shows, no type is immune
from their effect. Thus, while most American colleges and universities are proceeding in traditional ways and some categories are
more resistant to change than others, the movement of academic
reform through waves of innovation and subsequent imitation
means that eventually all institutions will be influenced whether they
wish to be or not.

Table 6

PERCENT OF INSTITUTIONS OFFERING ONE OR MORE
NON-TRADITIONAL PROGRAMS

Institution	Percent
Universities	
public	40
independent	50
religious	10
Four-Five Year Colleges	
public	27
independent	30
religious	24
Two-Year Colleges	
public	39
independent	26
religious	23

As expected, the development and implementation of new programs encountered a number of obstacles. The percentages of the 1185 respondents (mostly central academic administrators) expressing institutional concern about various difficulties were: lack of funds, 41 percent; difficulty in assessing nonclassroom learning, 40 percent; institutional concern about its academic standards, 34 percent; faculty resistance, 32 percent; problems of budgets based on full-time equivalent units, 25 percent; lack of interest within the institution, 21 percent; suspicion of passing fad, 20 percent; lack of approved examination or other assessment technique, 19 percent; acceptance of graduates into advanced education or graduate schools, 18 percent; no evident demand or need for such developments, 15 percent; recruitment of appropriate faculty, 13 percent; recruitment of students, 12 percent; lack of interest among institution's constituency, 12 percent; inadequate preparation of students, 12 percent; accreditation, 10 percent; licensing and certification, 9 percent; employers' concern about graduates' qualifications, 7 percent; other, 6 percent.

The Commission seeks to help institutions overcome these problems and adapt their structure and governance to new needs through the following recommendations on the reshaping of colleges and universities. It has divided these recommendations into three major groups, each of which has a distinctive focus. The first set concerns the general reconstruction or reframing of policies in American higher education as a whole. The second changes focus and relates to the individual institution which wishes to create and operate major new programs of service. Finally, the third considers finance as an essentially separate question since the issues which it raises relate to both the overall system and the individual institution.

Reshaping the System

The Commission addresses the first of these recommendations to all educators and lay citizens but particularly to curricular theorists who define the principles on which sound educational articulation should be based.

11. Careful attention should be given to articulation among earlier, higher, and adult education, particularly in relation to non-traditional study.

The formal educational system of this country has been pieced together out of various units of instruction, some of them imported from abroad (such as the kindergarten and the Ph.D. program) and others created here (such as the four-year high school and the community college). By a process which owes more to improvisation than to deliberate design, these units have been constructed into a ladder, up which the individual climbs from the entry rung in nursery school at the age of two until the culminating doctorate in the mid-twenties or later. The spare simplicity of this analogy is belied by the intricacies of reality, but the concept of the educational ladder has become fastened firmly in the American consciousness as the only appropriate way to shape the system.

For a half century, educators have been concerned about the articulation of the units of this system—that is, with providing a smooth progression from one unit to another not merely for those students who fit a hypothetically normal pattern of interests and abilities but also for individuals who fall outside this common pattern. Profound changes have occurred as a result, with the community college as one example. But further variations and alterations among the units and the awards they provide are being organized or are under discussion, among them the three-year baccalaureate, the three-year medical school after the four-year baccalaureate, the "middle college" combining the last year or two of high school with the two-year curriculum of the junior college, and the upper-division college offering three-year professional or specialized degrees. The plans and proposals are complex; their permutations and combinations bewildering; and their potential for change striking. There is little doubt that some will win substantial recognition and perhaps wide acceptance. But all are piecemeal approaches. The proponent of the three-year baccalaureate, for example, is likely to take the rest of the educational system for granted while he concentrates on the single reform he wishes to effect. The two-year–college partisan may do the same. Yet the limitations of single solutions must be recognized.

The Commission is far from being opposed to segmental

approaches, for it seeks diversity and variety rather than a rigid and crystallized system and recognizes that many people can be passionately motivated pioneers only within restricted spheres. But comprehensive thought must be given to the whole system of education, and in particular the single-ladder concept must be abandoned. The notion that all the education that really counts can be organized into a graded system which begins in the early years of life and runs sequentially and unhesitatingly for sixteen or more years (what some call a "front-loaded system") is no longer in accordance with observable facts. In its place, another idea is evolving as was pointed out in Chapter Two: that the education of the individual is lifelong, and formal instruction should be available periodically throughout the lifespan.

In the United States, "lifelong learning" has often been used as a synonym for "adult education," but properly conceived the term should cover the whole span of life, including the early years. (The French call this idea *education permanente,* which some English-speaking people, particularly those in UNESCO and Council of Europe circles, translate directly as "permanent education," despite the unfortunate connotations of the phrase and its failure to convey the intended meaning.) The idea implies that the curricula of early education should be redesigned, since some subjects can best be learned in childhood, some in youth, and some in adulthood. It suggests that occupational education at every level of complexity should be reoriented to emphasize fundamentals more than particular applications and special tasks which the worker may not encounter until late in his career. In addition, it proposes that continuing and recurrent education should be tailored to the special circumstances of the individual's life.

Experiments are already being constructed to test the possibility of a continuum of learning within and outside the educational system to bridge present gaps in understanding between levels and units of the system. At the Institute of Education at Hamburg, an international group of scholars is embarking on a detailed study of the implications of the idea, particularly in the years of childhood and youth. In the United States the most substantial effort known to the Commission has been proposed in Wisconsin, where a task force appointed by the governor is working out the implications of *education permanente* for that state's educational system. According to its chairman, Charles Wedemeyer, the task force is to develop "a corollary system of education for all the people of the state, cradle to grave, meshed with all existing educational systems in the state, and drawing upon established public and private educational institutions, business, government, industry, and libraries for its major resources."

The development of such conceptions as these and their testing by experience at every level of lifelong learning will help higher education cope with change far more ably than it ever has before. They may also help students cope with institutions by providing clear articulation. A student nurtured in traditional forms of elementary and secondary education is bound to have great difficulty adjusting in college to non-traditional options that give him more flexibility, more independence, and more responsibilities for self-motivation than he has ever known before, just as a student who has become used to a broad range of learning possibilities in non-traditional schools will be stifled by the traditionalism of some colleges.

12. There should be continued experimentation with forms of non-traditional study which minimize the traditional rigidities of campus life: time (prescribed years of study); space (residence on campus); and systems of academic accounting (credits or honor points earned).

The formal educational system from beginning to end is based on the idea that groups of people can be instructed simultaneously for a set period of time, that by the laws of statistics they fall into a normal distribution of ability and of performance, that what they learn is capable of being added up to a given number of semester or quarter hour credits, that these credits are interchangeable with one another regardless of content (but vary in meaning under formal rules such as the one which dictates that one hour of class time equals two hours of laboratory work), and that the whole system is made coherent and manageable by being isolated from the external world and being operated in a separate and commonly shared geographic setting.

Such a systematized approach was perhaps inevitable, given the degree of efficiency and the size of the task made necessary by the egalitarian nature of American higher education. Fortunately, there is a long and healthy history of individuals and groups who have found ways to circumvent the system, and, as the Commission's studies show, at least a third of American colleges and universities have developed unconventional approaches more flexible than this system. The theoretical base for such approaches is now being laid so that the people who use them need no longer feel like rebels. A new set of terms and concepts is being developed, some of which represent very old ideas and all of which, like other innovations, will doubtless be carried to a cultish excess.

The Commission believes that the potential of these approaches outweighs the possibility of excess. The rigidities of time, space, and academic credentialing have worked directly, though often covertly, to foster elitism in higher education. The aims of education properly involve the achievement of competence, understanding, knowledge, and sensitivity. If attention is focused on diverse means to these objectives and not on rigid structure, many people not now thought to be "college material" can achieve these goals. John Carroll (1965) has shown, for example, that if a group of students are all taught in the same way, their distribution on measures of achievement for a given subject will fairly well replicate their distribution on measures of aptitude in the subject. Naturally some of them will do poorly. But if the nature, quality, and time devoted to instruction are appropriate to the interests and capacities of individual students, the correlation between the range of original aptitudes and that of achievement becomes less significant, and most of them can achieve the aims of instruction.

It has long been a cliche to attack the lockstep of education. Social ills are not solved by identifying them. It is necessary to discover their roots and to change action patterns which reinforce them. Such is the proper course for non-traditional education.

13. The distinctive pattern of non-traditional study in each of the major institutions of higher education—such as the community college, the small private college, the land-grant college, or the single- or multi-campus university—should be further explored and defined.

This subject has been addressed in discussions and publications of the organizations which represent higher education broadly, such as the American Council on Education, the American Association for Higher Education, the College Entrance Examination Board, the American College Testing Program, the regional accrediting associations, and the U. S. Office of Education. Yet the problems of each type of institution are sufficiently distinctive to require specialized attention. This recommendation is thus addressed particularly to the national, regional, and state associations of such institutions and is intended to reinforce their evident interest in non-traditional study through their general meetings, conferences, and commissions.

As noted earlier, in Commission meetings with representatives of these collegiate groups, each had lively and distinctive ideas not only about what is going on but also about how the future should be shaped. For example, large-scale multicampus institutions have shown a great deal of interest in external degrees and other forms of non-traditional study. So far, each campus has usually been encouraged to try innovative practices, with perhaps some sympathetic attention from the chancellor at budgetmaking time. Then, the non-traditional methods that succeed can be spread to the whole system and, in time, be widely diffused. An alternate policy, however, would be to identify one campus as the center of experimentation, thus concentrating and focusing innovation while allowing other campuses to go their own ways.

To take another example, the community college is certain to continue to be a major center of non-traditional study, adding new achievements to its already impressive ones. But in many cases, heavy emphasis on two-year programs (no matter whether transfer, general, or terminal) stands in the way of counseling, adult education, and community service functions. To be truly non-traditional, the institution evolving out of the old junior college must become a fifty-year college, not a two-year college. It must in time have programs and sequences of programs of almost any length, with students attending continuously or intermittently as they are motivated. The rigidity of the "lower-division" mentality and the movement "upward" to a full four-year–college status must both be avoided.

Four-year colleges are likely to have, at most, only one or two adult programs, sometimes peripheral, at best, to their regular programs. But even relatively small universities (with, say, eight to ten thousand students) may have from seven to twelve separately organized extension divisions and services, and larger universities are honeycombed with them. In major state universities, where adult education has become a pervasive rather than a concentrated function, three different forms of adult education service require coordination: the general extension division, which operates adult education facilities and tries to maintain some degree of all-campus comprehensive service; the Cooperative Extension Service, which originally concentrated on offering services to farm families but now has greatly broadened its coverage and the size of its staff; and a rapidly growing number of specialized services that focus on continuing education for specific professional or occupational groups or on operating facilities such as a radio or television station, a center for continuing education, or a community development program.

While a few universities have succeeded in coordinating these various domains, in most cases adult education policy is not set by any general academic board, and only the chancellor, president, provost, or other general officer has comprehensive supervision over the total institutional program of adult education. The Commission holds that adult education is an all-university responsibility and that these general officers and their assistants should exercise greater guidance and direction over all adult and other non-traditional programs than they have in the past. The Commission also holds that academic senates and their committees should take a much more active role than they now do in setting policy for all such programs.

These examples indicate what the Commission means when it says that non-traditional study has special implications for each institutional type. Although these implications were explored extensively at general and special meetings of the Commission and its committees, the Commission does not choose to offer more detailed prescriptions or recommendations because the associations of these various types of colleges and universities are already undertaking that task. They are to be commended for such efforts. The Commission hopes that productive results will soon be evident.

14. Inventories of current non-traditional arrangements,

programs, changes in structure, and credentialing should be under-
taken nationally within each level or segment of higher education.

The Commission's study of the supply of non-traditional
opportunities in public, independent, and religious institutions was
described briefly earlier. When this study is published, it will serve
as an invaluable source of information in itself as well as a baseline
for later studies. The Commission believes that some kind of a
continuing data base of this sort, suitably refined by continuing
experience, should be undertaken by the National Center for Educational Statistics or some other appropriate statistical unit of the
Department of Health, Education, and Welfare. The Educational
Amendments of 1972, already quoted, lay great emphasis on innovation and the creation of new non-traditional forms. Other
pieces of legislation on higher education, at various stages of formu-
lation or implementation, have the same emphasis. If some comprehensive and cumulative record of changes and developments is not
created and maintained, a great deal of money will be wasted by the
constant reinvention of already well-worked-out programs and by
ignorance concerning the institutions to which would-be pioneers
can turn for help.

15. Increased collaboration among existing institutions
should be encouraged, including that among public and private
institutions.

The divergent origins of the several types of colleges and
universities mean that they bring different backgrounds of thought
and resources to their students. The literature of higher education
has long stressed both the economies and the enrichments of opportunity resulting from collaboration among institutions. Non-traditional study offers yet another way to weave the fabric of American
higher education more tightly and particularly to diminish the
separation between public and private institutions. The collaborative thinking of administrators and faculty members as they develop
new ventures stimulates interinstitutional inquiries, comparisons,
planning, and cooperation which the mere fitting together of the
pieces of conventional programs can never create.

In its survey of the supply of non-traditional opportunities,
detailed information was obtained on 351 of the total 641 programs,

including their interinstitutional status. If these selected programs are as representative as they seem, most non-traditional study is still conducted by individual colleges and universities alone. Of the 351 programs, 58 percent were conducted by a single educational institution, 18 percent were operated cooperatively by two or more educational institutions, 16 percent were undertaken by an institution in collaboration with a business firm, social agency, or other noneducational organization, and 4 percent were offered by a combination of several kinds of institutions (another 4 percent gave no interinstitutional data). Collaborative programs are more common in public than in private institutions. In universities, for example, 49 percent of the programs of public institutions were collaborative in contrast with 32 percent of those sponsored by independent institutions. Among four-year colleges the comparable figures were 54 percent and 29 percent, and among two-year colleges, the difference was between 45 percent and 38 percent. The Commission hopes that when future surveys as advocated in the previous recommendation are undertaken, they will find significant increases in these percentages of collaborative programs.

16. Appropriate alterations in patterns of governance should be considered when non-traditional arrangements become significant either within an institution or among institutions.

The way American colleges and universities are governed has been fixed for many years. Overall responsibility and authority are allocated to a board of trustees, executive responsibility and authority to administrative officers, and control of academic matters and consultative rights in other matters to the faculty; student participation is absent or limited at all levels and ordinarily exists only as representation.

This well-recognized and traditional pattern has occasional but not numerous deviations, but now the introduction of new arrangements for learning in a single institution or in collaboration with other institutions suggests that changes within this governance pattern may be desirable as well as inevitable. The legislative role of each constituency deserves reexamination, as do traditional concepts of institutional independence within collaborative agreements. The task of bringing about the appropriate interrelationships is complex, yet unilateral decisions by one group within the institution or by one institution within a consortium cannot be expected to win acceptance from all the other members. Interlockings, mergings, representations of many sorts that create the instruments for decision-making are as crucial to the success of institutions as they are in consortia or even informal kinds of collaboration. All are bound to affect governance since they lead either to shared authority, direct assignment of authority to one party within the enterprise, or separation and dissolution.

There should be systematic study, therefore, of the impact on governance at institutions which have already developed non-traditional programs alone or in concert. For example, how does the governance of New York's Empire State College or of Minnesota's Metropolitan State College differ from that of traditional institutions? What changes in authority take place in institutions belonging to the Committee on Institutional Cooperation, the Association of Mid-Western Colleges, the Five-College Consortium in the Connecticut Valley, or other joint endeavors? These institutions offer clues as to the effects that non-traditional programs and cooperation have on trustee, administrative, and faculty relationships and on institutional sovereignty.

The American Association for Higher Education, with support from The Danforth Foundation, has established a cooperative program under which representatives of 75 consortia meet semiannually to share experiences and exchange information on developments in these collaborative efforts. This group might well be the agent to gather information on institutional sovereignty or make its knowledge on these matters widely known. Similarly, students of institutional governance should note the consequences for decision-making wherever major non-traditional programs are under way.

Adapting the Institution

Previous recommendations in this chapter primarily concern systems and consortia of institutions. Now the focus of the Commission's recommendations shifts specifically to the individual college or university as it plans and carries out non-traditional methods. In any such case, many local factors come into play, such as the size, complexity, and nature of support of the institution. As suggested earlier in this chapter, a multicampus, complex public university organizing non-traditional programs may have problems very different from those of a small, private, liberal arts college. The Commission tried to consider all the various possibilities and applications of policy, and here its recommendations seek to apply at least in general terms to every institution in which change is likely to occur.

17. The support of boards of trustees or regents, commissioners, presidents and other administrators, faculty senates and controlling committees, and student organizations should be actively sought in any efforts to introduce non-traditional forms into existing institutions.

As indicated above, there is little point in glossing over the fact that major innovations in program, in interinstitutional relationships, or in credentialing will significantly affect college and university structures and procedures of governance. It is imperative, therefore, that such innovations be planned and introduced with the full knowledge and support of all constituencies.

Boards of trustees, for example, should realize from the beginning that collaborative arrangements with other institutions may lead to a redefinition of their own responsibilities. They should realize also that non-traditional forms will naturally seem alien at first and will need time to prove their academic justification. Faculty members are similarly cautious about academic change, particularly because of what it can mean to their academic disciplines and professional careers. To embark on any innovation without their understanding, support, and active cooperation is to court disaster. And students, particularly today, are properly concerned about being involved in decision-making directly or indirectly whenever options are examined.

Leadership in persuading these constituencies that change is necessary and even desirable is the responsibility of the college or university president. The future of the institution literally hinges on his ability to influence trustees, faculty, students, lay citizens—in groups or as individuals—to support whatever the institution requires. Sometimes the persuasion relates to a specific program, sometimes to a philosophical conviction. Many times it means long hours of patient negotiation in defense of a principle. Persuasion is, in a very real sense, the only effective power the president has. He can summarily order things to be done and his orders are likely to be obeyed, but the result may be a Pyrrhic victory. Any idea, any program, any change of consequence must be accepted intellectually and emotionally by those who will be directly involved. Otherwise it has no true permanence. It will survive for a while but only under duress, and usually will disappear as soon as its proponent relaxes his vigilance. Nowhere is this more true than in his relations with the faculty.

18. Administrators and faculty groups should work together to encourage and foster the development of non-traditional systems of education.

The long tradition of higher education has created within each institution two forms of authority and responsibility: the *hierarchical* exercised by the administrators and the *corporate* exercised by the faculty. The Commission hopes that both sources of power can collaborate in developing new learning patterns and a broad range of choices for the student and avoid a single and ever more rigid fixation on the past. If the latter attitude becomes dominant, an increasingly sophisticated public will find adequate remedies, most likely by abandoning formal systems of education and using the alternate agents of learning which are proliferating in modern society.

Where power is divided, tensions are inevitably created and each party tends to create a stereotype of the other. Encouragingly, this may not be happening in the development of non-traditional programs. According to data from the 351 programs selected for intensive study, power over them is seldom lodged only in administrative positions. In 58 percent, for example, faculty committees have the same involvement as in conventional programs; in 22 percent they have at least some participation in policy-making, and in only 13 percent do they have little if any involvement (no information was available for the remaining 7 percent). And some administrators commented that faculty members are more involved with decisions concerning non-traditional programs than with conventional programs.

On most campuses, in short, the relationship between administrators and faculty members appears collaborative regarding these programs. The Commission hopes that this pattern does not change into a rigid and confrontational form. Collective bargaining procedures at colleges and universities are still enough in their infancy that the Commission hesitates to guess how extensive they will become, under what auspices they will occur, or with what content they will deal. But to whatever extent collective bargaining proceeds, it will presumably deal with such issues as membership in the faculty bargaining unit, conditions and places of work, and bases of compensation. Such matters obviously will affect the development of unconventional programs and may ultimately determine whether an institution can be innovative or whether it must stick forever to old patterns. The Commission hopes that the desirability of collaboration between administration and faculty on non-traditional study will continue to be recognized both on campuses which adopt collective bargaining procedures and on those which do not.

19. An institution designing a non-traditional program, particularly one leading to an external degree or some other evidence of substantial study, should relate such a program to its whole process of curriculum development.

If this recommendation is not followed, the new program is likely to fail. Merely shifting one component of instruction without thinking through and, if necessary, redesigning its relationship with the others will create problems which may ultimately be insoluble.

There are always great temptations to move swiftly, particularly in our modern public-relations-oriented world. The communications media are avid to report exciting efforts of all kinds even when their success is still unproved, while many innovators are eager to be first rather than best and are not at all hesitant about publicity. Everyone is in a hurry to get into the spotlight first, even before there has been time for prudent evaluations and judgments. Such practices are contrary to the very meaning and spirit of the profession of education, but the temptation to use them is great and many succumb. All a project needs for attention is novelty, color, promise, and preferably the possibility of controversy; thus what is featured and remembered most easily by the public is not necessarily the most important element of what is being tried.

The person who suffers most from the absence of solidly planned and developed programs is the prospective student. Among his or her expectations, two could be most seriously disappointed: first, that the non-traditional offerings are indeed different enough from conventional ones in material or in flexibility to meet individual needs, interest, and requirements; second, that these offerings form a flexible but intellectually rewarding whole rather than a motley collection of largely unrelated parts. The enthusiasm generated, particularly among students beyond traditional college age, could soon evaporate and change to apathy when their expectations are not met. A relatively small number of excellent non-traditional programs might emerge, but unable to overcome the disappointment and suspicion generated by inadequate ones, would be tarred by the stigma of the rest. Like any innovative movement, in short, non-traditional study may succumb to oversell and overreaction.

In designing a non-traditional program, therefore, particularly one intended to award an external degree or some other certificate indicating sustained study, it is essential to proceed through the whole process of curriculum development. Objectives must be identified. A suitable format pays attention to resources, leaders, methods, schedule, sequence of instruction, the processes of social reinforcement, the individualization of instruction, the roles and relationships of the various persons involved, the criteria and methods of evaluation, and the clarity of the whole design. Thought must be given to fitting this format into larger patterns of life by considering such matters as guidance, finance, the customary life style of the learner, and interpretation to various publics. When the plan is put into effect, it must be constantly readjusted to take account of emerging opportunities and problems. At the end, the results must be measured and judgments made about the changes required if the program is to be repeated.

Anything other than a systematic and thorough approach of this sort is less than the student has a right to expect and will inevitably keep non-traditional programs out of the mainstream of academic development within the institution and throughout higher education. They can easily become peripheral curiosities that add spice and humor to faculty club conversations, but remain isolated within the institution and the larger system and unlikely to figure significantly in their future.

20. Colleges and universities should put more emphasis on

the avenues they open to learning for its own sake and less on the earning of degrees; adult education which is free of credit should be encouraged; and employers should be made to show clear and justifiable reasons for requiring diplomas or degrees as prerequisites to employment.

As the Commission looks back over its two years of exploration and study, it is aware as never before of the growing obsession with the acquisition of academic degrees. They have steadily proliferated until now more than sixteen hundred different ones are awarded, and they increasingly overshadow the concept of learning for its own sake. The detailed mechanics of degree-granting are expensive and time consuming; it is safe to say that in many institutions they receive far more attention and resources than more important explorations of the learning process itself. The problems, for instance, of collating and measuring achievement, of evaluating academic divisions and programs, of strengthening old structures or providing new ones—all of these emphasize the degree as the criterion and goal rather than learning as an end in itself, learning that expands, enriches, or challenges the individual and adds meaning to his or her life.

In spite of the Commission's awareness of this long-term trend and its concern over this imbalance in institutional and national education purposes, it is forced to admit that it, too, has reflected the trend in most aspects of this report. Because of the great public attention devoted in the last two years to the external degree and to new ways of earning credit or credit equivalency, most of the Commission's discussion of non-traditional study has revolved around these two issues. Yet it did not intend to limit its concern to the opportunities of young people and adults for earning credentials and degrees, internal or external. Its interest in making this credentialing system more equitable and open, as illustrated by its sixth and fiftieth recommendations, should not overshadow its emphasis upon lifelong learning through continuing and recurrent education, whether credentialed or not, as expressed in its second recommendation.

The Commission holds that access is essential for more people of more types and with differing needs to more possibilities for education, which may or may not include the awarding of a degree. Present pressures to acquire a degree, such as those by employers and even educational institutions themselves, often constitute arbitrary demands for convenient ways of categorizing abilities without actually measuring them, and hence must be countered.

The Commission's study of educational demand shows clearly the desire of many adults for credit-free education and for learning as more than a means to improved economic status. The continuing education of adults has an old and distinguished tradition in American universities and has made a substantial impact on the lives of individuals, groups and institutions, and the nation itself. The effect of agricultural extension in not merely raising the productivity of agriculture but also in helping to change the whole nature of rural life is a dramatic example. Other evidence is provided by the recent survey undertaken by the Southern Association of Colleges and Schools of its 560 member colleges and universities (Andrews, 1973). It found that 415 or 74 percent of them offer adult, continuing, or extension programs, and that a large part of these programs emphasize knowledge for its own sake. For example, fully 36 percent of the institutions conduct conferences, workshops, short courses, or institutes, and at least 26 percent offer cultural enrichment programs.

But credit-free learning is still a stepchild in the American educational pattern, and it will continue to lack support and importance so long as eligibility for further education and for jobs, promotions, and more income is based on credits and credentials. And even in credit-bearing education, appropriate recognition can be given for achievement through certificates and other credentials short of a degree after the completion of a particular program of study or experience.

Colleges and universities should look carefully at the limitations on opportunity caused by their present emphasis on associate, baccalaureate and other degrees as their primary goals. A better balance than exists presently must be found between the function of degree-granting and straightforward, uncomplicated service to the learner. The degree, in and of itself, should continue to be a hallmark of accomplishment. But institutions could do much to shift the attention of students of all ages from degree-earning per se to learning as a lifelong process with degrees awarded when appropriate but otherwise deemphasized. And in so doing, they would also help to solve some of the enrollment problems with which they are already plagued, since they would be opening new doors to more students. Indeed, a considerably different sort of institution might well emerge from such a shift.

The Commission has no illusions about the time required to lessen the current demand for degrees or to change the emphases in academic institutions. But the movement toward non-traditional arrangements makes the present an unusually good time to point to the problem and to urge that solutions be sought. In the area of employer demands, however, the Commission feels that much more immediate action is possible and desirable. The foundation for such action has already been laid. In March 1971 in the case of *Griggs* v. *Duke Power*, the Supreme Court ruled by an 8–0 decision that the Duke Power Company could not exact educational requirements or test results—such as a high school diploma—of job applicants unless the need for the requirements could be demonstrably proven to the satisfaction of the Court. Henceforth, if employers cannot demonstrate that such credentials are required for successful performance of a job, the courts have no recourse but to find them at fault. Pressure on employers to reexamine their hiring restrictions will call for new initiatives from the academic community and from public and private agencies concerned with civil rights. State governments are already making progress in protecting their citizens from diploma or degree mills; they now need to give attention to protecting them from illegitimate reliance by institutions and employers on academic credentials.

21. Existing colleges and universities should make every effort to meet the academic needs of additional numbers and new types of students. If they feel they cannot take on such responsibilities, they should welcome, even encourage, the growth of new institutions either of collegiate type or of some new model.

The massive growth of community colleges and of new state universities in the past twenty-five years has been an expression of the will of the public, through government auspices, to broaden higher education to include new kinds of students and curricula as well as to serve the ever-increasing number of young people of the sort who have always gone to college. In the same period, other institutions under religious, independent, and proprietary auspices have also flourished. In such circumstances, the choices suggested by this recommendation were not difficult to make. If growth seemed wise, the money for it could usually be found. If new institutions seemed to be the answer, sponsors from the established system of higher education often helped create them. The president of an Ivy League university could serve as chairman of an action group to improve public higher education in his state; a consortium of public and private colleges could sponsor a new college; a public university could counsel and assist a group of community colleges.

Such cooperation may be limited now that institutional prerogatives and even institutional survival are at stake and institutional freedom of choice is more difficult. Yet the Commission believes that the decision about whether or not to meet new needs or serve new clienteles still should be open to every institution. A college which maintains that its mission is to provide a broad liberal education only to young people in their immediate postadolescent years and whose record indicates that it fulfills this mission excellently should not assume that the Commission expects it to respond to demands for occupational and "relevant" curricula or to construct programs for new groups of students such as adults or the educationally disadvantaged. Yet the Commission suggests that such a college should use its influence to help create new institutions or training programs which can serve these students.

22. Faculty chosen for new programs should be creative, willing to learn any new techniques required, and sufficiently flexible to make changes; and they should be helped to retain these qualities.

No other recommendation of the Commission is more important or more difficult to achieve than this one. Many people who are skeptical of the success of non-traditional study suspect that institutions interested in unconventional education will either use faculty members who are rigidly set in traditional ways of work or restrict others within such conventional structures that they will never perform effectively and efficiently in the freer world of non-traditional study.

A third Commission survey, undertaken by the Center for Research and Development in Higher Education and consisting of depth interviews of twenty-five leaders of non-traditional programs and institutions, indicates that their most persistent problem is getting institutional and faculty support for innovation and then selecting and maintaining a teaching staff appropriate for the program. One chief difficulty (and one which nobody knows very well how to solve) is to discover people who thrive on novelty and uncertainty. "People who appear to be academic radicals in conventional settings," said one president, "can be rather dramatically unnerved when they are put in a setting where they are no longer radicals. One of the things which the conventional educational structure does is make them dependent on having a conventional educational structure to lean on. When they don't have that, they can become surprisingly conservative." A dean at another institution spoke of "running point-blank into the conservative, ivory-tower attitudes that hide behind academic freedom." And a third administrator noted that "there are good people who just cannot function in situations where there is no structure" and noted that "there should be a graceful means of exit for any administrator, faculty member, or staff member" who is paralyzed by the freedom and flexibility of non-traditional study.

Another difficulty is the inability of faculty members to work efficiently within the new instructional systems which non-traditional study often requires, as when teamwork is needed to develop new materials. To overcome this problem, one university has put together teams which include an instruction design specialist, a communications specialist, a specialist in correspondence study, an educational psychologist, and a graphics specialist to develop packages of materials and teach the faculty how to use them or how to advise students in their use. At another institution, a so-called planning period has been used in large part to train faculty in the new techniques they need, thus following Alexander Pope's recommendation that "men should be taught as though you taught them not." In still other institutions, training has been requested by the faculty after it encountered problems.

But, of course, in some cases training has been neither offered nor requested, the assumption being that faculty status conferred omnicompetence. "We need an intensive in-service training of faculty in terms of pointing to these new frontiers and definite techniques and to help them have respect for autonomy and the individual learner," stated the director of one program. Many another would agree with him. In fact, one of the most thoughtful and experienced leaders in all of non-traditional study is much alarmed by evidence of a widespread belief that "one can set up a program . . . by putting together a few counselors and making available all the resources that exist." He comments that "I don't think that's going to lead to an academic program of any quality at all." The Commission warmly agrees.

23. Although the core teaching in a non-traditional program must be done by full-time faculty members if it is to be an integral part of the work of the sponsoring institution, a college or university should enrich both its program and its community relationships by using highly qualified part-time teachers or leaders.

The majority of existing non-traditional programs already bear out this recommendation, though in varying degrees. While 5 percent of the 351 programs examined in detail by the Commission provided no information on the sources of their faculty, the distribution of faculty members in the others is indicated in Table 7.

These data suggest a heavy involvement of the regular professoriate, a relatively minor employment of full-time faculty specifically for the programs, and enough community-based instructors to bring in some additional diversity of viewpoint. The new flexibility that should be a hallmark of America's educational future makes necessary the inclusion not only of a wide circle of part-time students but also a great body of part-time faculty hitherto considered peripheral under such titles as "adjunct professor," "lecturer," or "field staff." These men and women in most cases are as well qualified by academic background to teach as their more traditional colleagues, except that their major careers are in scientific, technical, business, or cultural endeavors. Such community faculty members are not only necessary to cope with the impending expansion of numbers of students and variety of programs; they are desirable in terms of the broader dimensions of experience and wisdom they can inject into education.

Much non-traditional study involves a different and more personal relationship between faculty member and student, always highly prized but now even more valued because of the increasing

Table 7

SOURCES OF FACULTY IN 351 SELECTED
NON-TRADITIONAL PROGRAMS

Source	Programs with Majority of Faculty in Category	Programs with Minority of Faculty in Category	Programs with No Faculty in Category
	Percent		
Regular faculty who also teach conventional programs	62	17	16
Separate faculty engaged for the program alone	13	18	64
Special instructors from the community	16	39	40
Other (retired; graduate students; faculty from elsewhere)	4	3	88

importance of guidance and counseling in helping the individual move toward his own particular educational goals. "Regular" faculty can provide such advisement from one point of view but community faculty can do so from another. In non-traditional education, both are vital.

Community faculty members can also do a great deal to destroy the separatism which walls many colleges and universities from the communities they seek to serve. In highly specialized professional schools and graduate departments, professors and their proteges maintain contacts after the students' academic years, and some high-prestige liberal arts colleges maintain the active and articulate involvement of their general alumni. But many other institutions find their only continuing contact with the public to be the interpretation provided by sportswriters and commentators. The aims of academic life, as they change through the years, need constant reinterpretation, just as shifts in the outside community need to be expressed within the walls of the college and university. The community faculty helps bridge the gap, opening up the enclave of the campus even as it builds public understanding and support for the academic way of life.

24. Systems of faculty reward and promotion should not discriminate against the person who teaches in non-traditional programs.

In institutions which are wholly unconventional, the problem suggested by this recommendation does not arise with the strength or complexity that it does in institutions which have both conventional and unconventional programs operating side by side. It is true that a non-traditional college or university always has special problems with faculty members who do not want to be typecast, who grow weary of being outside the traditional system, or who are troubled by some other aspect of the institution, such as its small size or its distinctive reputation. In general, however, it lacks the invidious differences in status, rewards, and morale found in an institution supporting both non-traditional and traditional—and often competing—programs.* The Commission believes that, unless careful plans are laid in advance and subsequently enforced by vigilant administrators, discrimination in faculty rewards and promotion tends to operate against non-traditional programs, particularly when "publish or perish" is part of the institution's tradition.

It is only fair to note that in some cases, particularly with short-term, specially funded programs, the situation may be reversed. One president interviewed in the Commission's survey pointed with vigor to the pitfalls of such reverse differentiation: "In my experience, the surest way to surround non-traditional experiments with faculty hostility is to give those programs a richer mixture of dollars and personnel than the conventional programs. Since new ideas are threatening in themselves, then typically if we give most faculty smaller classes and more released time we are really asking for the faculty members who aren't involved in the

---

* Myrtle Jacobson provides an extensive and well-documented case study of these differences in *Night and Day* (Metuchen, N.J.: Scarecrow Press, 1970, pp. 149–208).

experiment to multiply their anger." The Commission thus warns
of possible harm in either direction.

25. *Admission of students to non-traditional programs should
be based on new kinds of examining procedures or more flexible
and interpretive application of criteria.*

A major incentive for creating non-traditional programs is
to reach more kinds of students, as the Commission's survey of these
programs has revealed. In dealing with varied groups, a college or
university should set up special admissions requirements, and many
of the 351 programs selected for special analysis have done so. The
admissions requirements are complex. As Table 8 shows, relatively few
of the programs require applicants to meet any of the usual criteria
for admission. By and large they are "open" rather than restrictive.

The large number of "other" responses included, in order

Table 8

ADMISSIONS REQUIREMENTS REPORTED

Requirement	Percentage of Programs
High school diploma or equivalent	47
Satisfactory scores on standardized examinations	11
Minimum age: 16 or younger	6
17 or 18	11
19 or 20	2
21 to 25	2
25 or over	2
Meets state education code requirements	7
Completion of lower-division work	7
Low socioeconomic background	7
Certain rank in high school class	4
Sex (men only or women only)	3
Particular ethnic background	2
Other	34

of frequency, no admissions requirements, the same requirements as for regular programs, proof of special skills or particular occupational experience, particular handicaps such as physical disability or incarceration, desire to learn and self-motivation, interviews, recommendations, and approval from faculty members or other agencies. This heterogeneous situation should continue even as generalized batteries of entrance examinations for such programs are developed. The Commission suggests only that the criteria used for admission should be flexible and applied with adequate attention to the qualities required to fulfill the objectives of the program.

26. New possibilities for campus residential arrangements which can provide an adjunct to learning, primarily for adult students, should be explored and tried.

To a very marked extent, non-traditional study has moved away from the campus. For example, the principal locations of learning activities in all 641 programs studied by the Commission are listed in Table 9.

Table 9

PRINCIPAL LOCATION OF LEARNING IN
NON-TRADITIONAL PROGRAMS

	Percent
Main campus	35
Regional learning or extension center	13
In the field	13
Business or industrial site	7
Community center, agency, or library	6
Home	5
Other location	10
Multiple locations	11

The Commission spent considerable time discussing and sometimes disagreeing on the values of campus residence for traditional students in traditional programs as well as for students in new programs. It could not avoid the current debates about changes in the goals, organization, and life styles of campus residence for traditional students; neither could it neglect the financial problems facing many colleges and universities which have long-range commitments to amortize the costs of student residences, even when students refuse to live in them. Yet the Commission ultimately focused attention on two issues: the principle of interpersonal relationships as an important part of learning, and how, in a non-traditional program, residence on campus can be a practical reality and a benefit to the learner.

Non-traditional education should not be interpreted as opposing campus residence, since learning is enhanced by interaction with others and by the interplay of human minds. Though solitude is often appropriate, so is exploration of ideas with others, and there is no question that the conditions arising when people live together with a common academic purpose can support and strengthen the learning process. But the idea that the classic pattern of four nine-month years of residence constitutes the only acceptable way of achieving the values of interaction needs to be reconsidered. Scholars educated in England are great champions of "residence," but even Oxford and Cambridge require for the baccalaureate only 72 weeks spent somewhere in the university's vicinity, whereas the classic American pattern requires a total of 144 weeks.

The Commission readily agreed, as was mentioned previously, that the use of residential facilities should be increased throughout the calendar year by making them available in various ways to non-traditional students, including adults. In order to enhance and strengthen the learning process, opportunities for short-term residence of adults on campuses, such as special conferences, weekend seminars, or vacation workshops, can be greatly expanded. Such opportunities can become one part of the recommended growth of recurrent education for adults.

27. Interruption of study on a planned basis should be accepted by educators and prospective employers as a potentially educational experience for students who elect it.

Most American colleges and universities, whether or not they approve of interrupted study, have had to accommodate "stopping out," as the Commission learned from the 1,182 institutions whose policies on this issue are categorized in Table 10.

The idea of a cohort of students entering college together, proceeding systematically through four years, and then maintaining for the rest of its life an identity as a formal class still has great meaning in many four-year colleges, particularly the older ones. There is no question that strong emotional ties to the institution are made even stronger thereby, as evidenced by the annual ritual of college class reunions. Even in such colleges, however, the "year

Table 10

POLICIES REGARDING INTERRUPTED STUDY

Policy	Percent
Continuous registration or progress is expected	17
Dropping in and out is facilitated but not encouraged	48
Neither practice is encouraged nor discouraged	28
Dropping in and out is encouraged	4
No information	3

abroad" concept (to name but one example) has become an acceptable interruption of on-campus study and is now supplemented in some places by comparable periods of residence off the campus for other purposes.

One result of informal interruption of study is that between one-quarter and one-half of the students in even the most highly selective and prestigious colleges are not graduating with the class they originally joined. They go off and do something else: work, wander, engage in military service, join such organizations as the Peace Corps or VISTA, or follow their inclinations in other ways. Later many of them return; in the types of colleges referred to, about 90 percent eventually finish their degrees.

In addition, cooperative education—alternate periods of work and study—provides many benefits not only by providing access to education but also by helping the individual develop a sense of maturity as well as assimilate knowledge and skills. Sometimes the work period is, intentionally or not, an escape for some students from the monotony of prolonged study. In other cases, it provides integration between study and employment. To quote from a pamphlet issued by England's Council for National Academic Awards, such periods "give the students the opportunity of applying in a work situation what they learn during their periods in college, and of seeing how industrial and commercial organizations operate. As their course progresses, they are able to carry out more responsible tasks in the firm, and in many cases they can make a useful contribution well before the end of their training periods."

The growth of the cooperative education movement in this country, especially in recent years and with the active encouragement of the National Commission for Cooperative Education, has shown conclusively an increasing acceptance of this non-traditional approach to learning. As of 1970, 225 colleges and universities were offering cooperative programs on 235 different campuses, and many more were being planned. Nor are the educational programs confined to vocational needs. In 1954, forty-six different curricula were being offered; by 1970 this number had risen to 165 and included much more representation than before in the liberal arts, education, actuarial science, or criminal justice, to mention only a sampling. (See Knowles, 1971, p. 344.)

Finally, there is good reason to believe that the student can benefit greatly by an interruption of his studies between high school and college if he so chooses, and that the interruption can be put to many good uses. The area of public service alone offers all sorts of opportunities not only for being actively involved where there are great manpower needs at lower levels but for channeling and directing some of the idealistic motivations of the young toward practical ways of fulfillment. Regular employment possibilities of an apprenticeship type are also important. These are only two out of several areas which can contribute to the general maturing of the individual, sharpen his motivations, and have educational significance besides.

The Commission feels that the lifelong educational achievement of many people might be much greater than at present if more of them had the planned opportunity or a counselor's encouragement to interrupt the lockstep of their age-graded and sequential study. The Commission readily admits that its convictions on this point are based on anecdotal rather than hard data and that much needs to be done in finding appropriate measurements of the educational impact of such types of experience, a point on which a broader recommendation will be made later. But the Commission does not doubt the desirability of these experiences.

28. Colleges and universities should work toward absorbing the external degree into the normal process of degree-granting instead of keeping it ancillary to their total program.

Many of the problems of non-traditional study discussed earlier are created or accentuated because it is held apart from the normal interplay of university relationships and the use of specialized services. This fact is particularly true of external degree programs which parallel the regular work of the university, as may be best illustrated perhaps by the comments of one person interviewed whose position in the central administrative group of a university provided unusually good perspective on such a program:

> In the area of integrating the external degree program with on-campus programs, we had some special problems, some of which we've solved and some we're still working on. There is always the problem of academic credibility—and it has been the primary problem. We approached it in several ways: first of all, we said that this program had to be more academically sound and stronger than ongoing programs because it's going to have to stand up against more careful scrutiny. So we began to develop procedures whereby we could hopefully ensure that credibility. This meant getting our faculty very much involved and particularly by creating a board to handle decisions. We were also concerned about getting procedures integrated through our regular recording system, our regular graduation procedures, and so forth.
>
> We began by developing a program that was quite independent as far as administrative details were concerned, and we kept it on a separate track from the ongoing programs of our graduate school office, our records office, and our admissions office. (We did stay with our regular admissions requirements, however.) Then after we got it operat-

ing with a few courses, we began a process of integrating these procedures into our regular procedures. So we are bringing it into the fold, although it didn't start that way. With a program such as ours, we needed to develop it independently at first. We wanted to save that innovative aspect of it and to get something ready first. But we didn't allow it to get so far afield that we couldn't get it integrated. We kept it separate for a time because that seemed to give us the most flexibility.

As this administrator suggests, integration of a non-traditional program into the normal operation of a college or university requires a great deal of tact and care so that the proper balance can be struck between freedom and responsibility both at the beginning and as it continues. The Commission believes, however, that such integration is essential and urges administrators and faculty members to encourage it.

Examining Finances

The third focus of the Commission in considering the re-shaping of colleges and universities was on finance. It was evident virtually from the start of its deliberations that insufficient knowledge exists for detailed suggestions. (However, see Appendix C for a proposed model for financing one particular mode of non-traditional study, the external degree.) The following recommendations, therefore, concentrate on remedying this situation so that better judgments can eventually be made.

29. Studies should be undertaken to get definitive answers to such questions as: (a) cost-per-student for providing units of instruction by various non-traditional methods; (b) cost-per-student and cost-per-program of non-traditional programs compared with traditional; (c) resolution of broad social issues related to financing non-traditional education; (d) advantages and disadvantages of institutional collaboration in handling endowment portfolios and in other financial matters.

Several inconclusive debates about non-traditional education center on funding, particularly on the source of funds and whether unconventional programs do or can lead to financial economies. The debates are inconclusive because insufficient data presently exist to substantiate any claims pro or con.

What financial data the Commission was able to gather indicate that current programs are receiving substantial subsidy. The primary sources of funding for the 351 programs analyzed in detail for the Commission are: student fees and grants (39 percent); institutional subsidy (25 percent); foundation or other outside grants (14 percent); a variety of other sources, such as state appropriations, industrial support, and community funds (13 percent); and a combination of sources (3 percent); with the remaining 6 percent unknown.

In comparing the operating costs of these selected programs with those of conventional programs in the same institutions, the general estimates ran as follows: generally similar costs (41 percent); generally lower cost (20 percent); and generally higher cost (17 percent); with no information available from the remaining 22 percent. This final figure is particularly interesting because it shows that about one-fifth of the respondents either did not have the information or did not wish to provide it. And the remainder of the data bear out the conclusion of the Commission that all too little is known about the cost, either direct or comprehensive, of non-traditional study.

The Commission places high priority on encouraging studies and analyses that would bridge this information gap. These studies are now being undertaken. They are examining three areas of information and judgment:

(1) The cost per student of providing units of instruction by each of several selected methods, such as independent study, home study, internship, and on-the-job training. The study involves the collection of data on costs incurred in actual programs by student-course enrollments and also a careful analysis using simulation techniques of the cost elements needed to deliver a given educational service to a given number of students during a given time unit. The costs per method can then be combined into systems or models of instruction for which total costs can be computed.

(2) Costing studies of each program of non-traditional education, based on both cost per student and cost per system, includ-

ing comparisons with similar programs of a traditional nature. Start-up, marginal, overhead, and replacement expenses will be determined.

(3) An examination by one or more economists of data relating to the broad social issues involved in financing non-traditional study and to questions of ethical choice. For example, should society encourage non-traditional study by providing relatively greater appropriations and gifts for it than are now given for conventional study? Should it encourage non-traditional students, many of whom are adults, by relatively low fees or generous aid or, conversely, should it take into account that older persons may be able to pay these fees because of being employed while studying part-time? These are but a few of the questions at issue.

Despite the need for these new analyses, the Commission suggests that institutions consider non-traditional approaches in the areas of management and finance that have already provided some evidence of success. For example, a few consortia of colleges are collaborating on maintenance and operational services such as purchasing materials, constructing buildings, library cataloging, and sharing computers. Similar collaboration on a broader scale has been shown to be possible by the Common Fund, in which 261 colleges and universities have pooled part of their endowment resources and are receiving a better income yield than they were individually accustomed to. Such cooperation is still a great unexplored area of considerable promise. The Commission believes that organizations such as the National Association of College and University Business Officers or the Association of Governing Boards of Universities and Colleges should, with foundation support, examine these financial matters speedily. Pointed advice on areas of possible economy and efficiency will assist not only the proper and stable growth of non-traditional education in its many forms but traditional education as well.

30. Alternative fee structures made necessary by non-traditional arrangements should be examined to provide assurances that academic institutions can find adequate income under such arrangements.

The Commission believes that one of the most serious problems affecting the development of non-traditional study involves finding new ways to charge for services. A very large part of the income of colleges and universities—two-thirds or more in many private institutions—is tuition payments. If an institution moves toward non-traditional bases for awarding degrees or even for offering programs, it must either find equivalences for credit points or fashion a new form of assessment—as has been done by the special-degree programs for adults. Public institutions, whose income is ordinarily determined on a full-time–student (or equivalent) basis, have a similar problem in that some formula of payment must be devised that guarantees adequate support. The whole issue deserves the most careful attention of experts in educational finance. Alternate fee structures cannot be avoided when major educational changes occur.

Quite apart from this need for new fee structures, the Commission is deeply concerned, especially in the current period of less rather than more support to the individual and the institution, over the attitude of federal, state, and local governments toward part-time students. Many legislative proposals and enactments concentrate almost solely on the full-time student both in relation to assisting the institution and in establishing scholarship benefits. This discrimination against the part-time student must be ended, as must institutional restrictions on services and aid for their less-than-full-time students.

In light of the variety of influences that non-traditional education is beginning to have on the structure of our existing academic institutions, the recommendations of the Commission in this area take on a tone of immediacy and urgency. This note has not come about by chance. It is the inevitable result of the Commission's realization that the pace of change in education, as in all major areas of need in our society, continues to be swift; that action to guarantee orderly progress and the structures to direct and assess such progress in the midst of this swiftness are necessary; and that a sufficient degree of change has already occurred for us all to recognize ways to reshape these structures.

4

EXAMINING
ALTERNATIVES

Almost as many Americans seek some form of education outside the established educational system as within it. Presently this country has a combined school and college population of about sixty million students; in addition, more than twenty million people are participating in some kind of out-of-school program. The investment of time these people are making in the programs they have elected is direct evidence of a demand and hence of psychological need.

Evidence of another kind of need, social need, is provided by statistics on the total educational attainment of the population. About forty-eight million people over the age of twenty-five have not completed high school, and millions of people younger than twenty-five have dropped out of the school system at some point along the way. In a technological era, with increasing demands for high-level proficiency, successful adult functioning can be seriously impaired unless skills are increased.

The need is by no means confined to those who lack a high school diploma. Even highly trained professional people require resources for review and retraining in their own fields. At the other end of the age scale are the preschoolers, especially those in poverty areas, whose early development could be enhanced by well-developed systems to stimulate learning either at home or through such arrangements as day care centers.

There is, then, a very large group of people outside the formal structure of education with obvious educational needs. If society is to develop mechanisms to help meet these needs, an essential early step is to analyze the populations reached by the nonformal systems. The Commission has made a beginning through its study of educational demand and its call for further study in Recommendations Nine and Ten. But level of student interest is not the only subject on which knowledge is needed. We need to know where and when instruction can be given—on the job, at home, in churches or moviehouses or libraries or community centers—and the best means of instruction: books, lectures, tapes, films, radio, cable or open or closed television, cassettes, computer terminals, organized community experiences, or combinations of these. In the present chapter, the Commission turns to what is already known about these alternate systems of learning, what role they should play in non-traditional study at large, and what more must be learned about them.

Education outside the classroom is by no means neglected at the present time, as shown by the large number of people already engaged in it. Present programs now provided outside traditional academic structures extend from Sesame Street through refresher courses for professional specialists and include Head Start, Follow Through, private corporations operating under "performance contracts," street academies, the Job Corps, the Neighborhood Youth Corps, proprietary schools, correspondence schools, USAFI courses in the armed services, labor union schools or workshops, and in-service programs by business and industry.

Some of these out-of-school efforts are impressive. Sesame Street and its later companion, The Electric Company, are prime examples: clearly, great imagination, wide talent, and solid preparation have gone into their development. The quality of their material is far above that of most educational television. Substituting an informal format for the usual didactic approach, they convey their message with a freshness seldom found in ETV shaped within conventional educational molds. The combination of extensive financial support, high-quality material, professional production, and effective delivery unconstrained by old habits of educational thought is powerful. In contrast, however, many other educational television productions are small in concept and indifferently successful.

In-service instruction provided by business, industry, and labor unions presents a similarly mixed picture with respect to quality. The best are outstanding but limited in the numbers they reach. Inevitably some are mediocre or worse.

Correspondence courses are sometimes done well, but the field has been plagued by unscrupulous operators, and efforts to monitor and control their activities have not been wholly successful. And the user is thus in a highly vulnerable position. Even the best schools can seldom put great resources into developing materials of high quality, and interaction with the student is severely limited.

The present scene, then, is marked by a commendable diversity of approaches but also by a troubling range of quality. Most individual efforts lack the resources of money and talent to achieve a high degree of effectiveness; their approach is piecemeal; their continuity non-existent.

One important feature of out-of-school teaching is that unorthodox instruction can be geared to the particular subject matter and the circumstances in which it is offered. The formal education system has accumulated extensive beliefs and traditions about the way educational needs ought to be served, and the forms and processes common to colleges and universities may be more readily modified or discarded by programs developed outside them. Fresh approaches are desirable in themselves because they extend educational opportunity but also because they may ultimately feed into the orthodox system as an important side effect.

The Commission's recommendations are based on this belief. They relate to two intertwined but separable problems: first, improved use of alternate *structures and systems* to expand total educational possibilities for students, and second, widespread use of new technological tools and devices as alternate *methods* of instruction.

Alternate Systems

Sporadic efforts have been made since 1926 to develop a conceptual framework which would embrace and classify all alternate systems of education. The results have been no more than listings of major types with no unifying concept such as that which the idea of the educational ladder provides the formal system.

Among the dominant sponsors of these alternate forms of education are those listed in Table 11, which indicates, from the Commission's study of educational demand, where American adults are currently engaged in learning activities and the estimated number of these adult learners.

These figures deal only with adult part-time students, but many alternate systems also serve young people below the age of eighteen, a fact largely ignored by educators concerned only with the formal academic system of kindergarten through college. Any inventory of childhood learning should take account of music lessons, the Sunday school class, the scout troop, the summer camp, the recreation center, the Y, the 4-H Club, the public library, the museum, the self-directed hobby, and many other consciously planned experiences which boys and girls undertake on their own initiative or at the suggestion of other people.

Society has excellent factual information on the amount and kind of schooling it provides but not about the amount and kind of education. One major reason is that in many cases education is a peripheral function of the institutions which offer it. Another is the difficulty in sometimes distinguishing education from their other functions. The frontier between learning and such other institutional purposes as therapy, recreation, aesthetic experience, healthful living, and religious feeling is often impossible to define exactly, but this does not mean that many organizations do not provide important educational services. While schools, colleges, and other institutions of the formal academic system bulk large on the horizon because they concentrate their efforts on educating primarily full-

Table 11

SOURCES OF ADULT LEARNING ACTIVITY

Sponsor	Number of Learners (in millions)	Percent of Learners
Academic institutions, such as high schools and colleges	7.4	22.9
Industry and employers	5.9	18.4
Self-study	5.4	16.9
Community organizations, such as YMCA	2.8	8.7
Religious institutions	2.0	6.3
Government agencies	1.8	5.5
Proprietary and correspondence schools	1.7	5.3
Private tutors	1.4	4.4
Museums, galleries, performing arts studios	0.7	2.3
Recreation and sports groups	0.7	2.3
Other organizations or no response	2.2	7.0

time students, the education performed by alternate systems is everywhere diffused in the lives of the people. That, in fact, is its greatest contribution.

Because it was patently impossible for the Commission to explore in depth every type of alternate approach, it chose out of several equally worthy of attention only one to discuss in detail— the public library. Others are included in later and more generalized recommendations.

31. The public library should be strengthened to become a far more powerful instrument for non-traditional education than is now the case.

This recommendation is directed not only to public officials and public librarians themselves but also to college and university faculty members and administrators who could work productively with them in developing non-traditional study opportunities at the postsecondary level. Public libraries have too long been regarded as passive conveyors of information or recreation, available when needed, but not playing, or expected to play, active roles in the educational process. Their vast capabilities have often been ignored. In truth the public library is literally a college around the corner. It was originally conceived by Benjamin Franklin to be the primary community resource for individual intellectual growth. It is a free institution where the individual has open access to great quantities of information. It exists in great numbers, possesses the materials of knowledge, has a public service staff, and is a referral point to other resources within the educational network.

There are close to ten thousand public libraries in the United States, and some thirteen hundred of them maintain an additional forty-nine hundred branch libraries. Their total book holdings are estimated to be in the neighborhood of 319,000,000 volumes. In recent years, a total of almost 850,000,000 volumes has been circulated annually to more than fifty million registered borrowers.

In addition to their book resources and unestimated additional holdings of periodicals, microfilms, sound recordings, films, and other nonbook materials, many libraries provide special rooms for public meetings and film viewings, study carrels, and facilities for the use of videotape, cable television, and other educational media. Interlibrary loans allow libraries throughout the country to obtain books for lending that they do not have in stock.

Librarians themselves are also an educational resource. In the 1968 Office of Education survey of public libraries which serve populations of more than twenty-five thousand, 1,057 libraries responding reported a total of 45,636 full-time employees, more than twenty percent of whom held at least fifth-year degrees in librarianship. All librarians graduating from accredited library schools have training in reference and bibliography, and many have academic specialties in which they maintain interest and competence.

Yet the strong and constructive effort of public libraries to build their own programs of services for individuals and groups and to collaborate with other agencies lags far behind the need for such services. The American Library Association (1972) recently issued the report of a special committee which reviewed the past with devastating frankness and set forth a bold program for the future. This document makes four clusters of recommendations designed to, first, achieve a better understanding of the public library in the community; second, stimulate a broad program of research which will undergird effective performance; third, support continued efforts to disseminate this research and embody its results in proto- type programs; and fourth, mount an intensive educational effort to help librarians know how to accomplish new goals by non-tradi- tional means. The Commission applauds and endorses this effort.

One very important service of the library warrants special mention here. The public library can be particularly supportive for people who are working for external degrees or other non-tradi- tional credentials as well as for those who are planning such pro- grams. Programs of this sort are already under way in White Plains, Boston, San Diego, Louisville, New York City, Dallas, St. Louis, and elsewhere, and several states have pooled services to enhance the availability of material. To give but one example, in several cities the public libraries are furnishing information about the Col- lege Level Examination Program and are assisting readers to find the books and other materials they need to prepare for these and other examinations.

As non-traditional study progresses, it will create problems but also enhance opportunities for public libraries. Demands for books and other materials and for help in finding them will grow. Interlibrary collaboration will increase and a large number of multicounty and other area libraries will probably be necessary. Changes in library architecture may be required to provide study centers, meeting rooms, and carrels. Librarians will have to counsel not only the students of programs but also their planners. Multi- system borrowers' cards may be necessary, and this fact will give rise to changes in fiscal support. Conflicts over goals will be sharp- ened; those who favor the library as a cultural center or as a place for undirected reading, recreation, and information-giving may feel threatened, particularly if budgets are not increased to make possible the achievement of all desired aims.

If the problems encountered in these programs can be solved —if the necessary funds are forthcoming, if staffs are prepared, information is disseminated, coordination is provided, and educators are made aware of potentialities for service—then libraries will no longer be merely extensions of educational programs but active planners and collaborators in them. The aim of public libraries to provide unlimited knowledge is in total harmony with the aim of non-traditional education: to provide unlimited opportunity. The possibility for joining the two should not be permitted to pass by quietly.

32. The persons who direct or certify the quality of alternate systems should continue to examine their policies and practices to be sure that sound education is being provided by them.

Many people believe firmly that the quality of education in alternate systems, particularly in programs operated by industry or commerce, is higher than that offered in schools and colleges. Anecdotal evidence can be presented that both supports and attacks this conclusion. Nobody has conclusive data on the point—particularly since, for the most part, alternate systems do not share with academic education the same patterns of evaluation and accreditation.

But alternate systems are not wholly free from external control. Some of them, operating either on their own initiative or in response to outside stimulation, have established both public and private ways to validate the quality of their work. In a few cases, particularly for those systems engaged in vocational education or designed to operate at a profit, both federal and state regulation exists, though it is spotty both in coverage and in the vigor of its administration. Also specialized accrediting associations, such as the National Home Study Council, the Accrediting Commission for Business Schools, and the National Association of Trade and Technical Schools, are making efforts to maintain or upgrade the quality of practice. Their task is certainly not easy, particularly when the profit motive is strongly involved or when a field of work is changing rapidly.

In the alternate systems, as in the formal academic system, the highest quality educational service should be sought. The Commission found itself wondering whether this effort is always made. The prevailing rule, often unsatisfactory in its application, is: Let the learner beware! To take but one example, many American proprietary schools employ salesman-representatives who are paid on the basis of the number of students they enroll. Even with the best possible selection, training, and supervision, can they be effective counselors if compensated on this basis? In Europe, the answer is resoundingly negative. In fact, Denmark, France, and Germany, forbid such schools to have representatives at all.*

Thus while government agencies and accrediting associations may intervene to maintain quality in alternate systems, primary control must be exercised by those who administer them. The teachings of a church; the instruction furnished by business, labor, or government to its own employees; the learning provided by voluntary societies to their members or to the public; the instruction offered by a private tutor or studio—these and many other systems of education lie, except in extreme cases, beyond the reach of the law and are amenable only to voluntary policing efforts. These efforts must begin internally.

33. The initial and continuing professional training of those who teach in alternate programs of education should include the concepts and techniques of non-traditional study.

Excellent training is important not only for faculty in collegiate non-traditional programs but for instructors in alternate systems. Extensive preparation of these lay leaders, such as Sunday School teachers, Red Cross instructors, and sponsors of youth groups, has been going on for a long time and some unconventional means have been adopted. Such people usually receive their guidance and direction from full-time professionals, many of whom, however, have never had any formal training to help them carry out their own work. Some of this training can occur in the preservice years: all pastors, for example, know that they must counsel and provide educational services for both adults and children and must therefore know how to respond to the desires and demands of both groups. In some alternate systems, however, staff training must be

---

* The French law on the matter is highly explicit: "It is prohibited to perform acts of canvassing or to delegate representatives for the account of educational bodies. The act of canvassing is constituted by the fact of visiting the domicile of private persons or visiting the place of work in order to bring about the signature of an educational contract."

on an in-service basis. A businessman, an armed services officer, or a health or welfare worker may not realize until years after he has left college that he will be assigned to educational duties. Any such person needs preparation for his new responsibilities just as much as does the college faculty member or administrator involved in non-traditional study.

But the choice is not really between preservice and continuing education. Each can supplement the other. In those systems in which teaching is merely a potential future option, its nature should be pointed out in a general way during preservice preparation but details can be left for later training. In those systems in which formal teacher training is appropriate for all workers, more should be offered before they enter service, although the changing life of the community and of the profession will require continued updating throughout their careers. The faculties of professional schools which train workers in alternate systems of education and the supervisors of continuing education programs thus have large responsibilities in disseminating the ideas of non-traditional education.

34. Creative ways should be found for coordinating the work of alternate systems with the academic system of education.

Libraries, museums, symphonic groups, business and industrial corporations, profit-making electronics and communications organizations, and military establishments are among the agencies which offer to people of all ages a great panoply of educational possibilities, sometimes greater in size and diversity and sometimes higher in quality than those presented more formally by educational institutions. A welding of all these would greatly expand individualized opportunity.

The learning resources of a community or region, together with those of the federal government, must be coordinated for effective use. A few years ago, the chairman of the Commission (Gould, 1970, p. 92) coined the term "communiversity" as a way of expressing this collaboration between institutions of higher learning and community agencies both in conducting ongoing programs, such as cooperative education, and in coping with special community and national problems. This report is not the appropriate place to repeat his full discussion, but the idea does have special applications for non-traditional education.

The development of non-traditional study increases the possibility of involvement between cultural and social agencies and educational institutions, as in the example of cooperation between public libraries and universities. Informal and formal systems of learning are drawing together. This collaboration is already evident from the Commission's survey of non-traditional programs. Of the 351 selected programs analyzed in depth, 20 percent were being carried out as part of a cooperative arrangement with one or more alternate systems. Such involvement, with proper monitoring, can lead to beneficial results on both sides.

A great deal of this coordinated effort has occurred, and should occur, as a result of purely local initiative and support. Major public problems, regardless of how national or international their scope may be, are rooted in local and regional communities and in the states. Solutions to urban blight, poverty, poor housing, over-population, deprivation of the essential rights of man—all these and others require the local involvement of the universities and the knowledge they can provide, as did the problems of rural life.

But just as the land-grant universities' aid to rural life stemmed from federal and state funds, so can collaborative effort in such areas as health, housing, poverty, and the general betterment of society. An excellent example is the program administered under Title I of the Higher Education Act of 1965, which in 1970–1971 supported 1,566 educational projects in forty-eight states. Congress set forth the goal of this program as "assisting the people of the United States in the solution of community problems . . . by making grants to strengthen the community service programs of colleges and universities"; and while the Title has always been funded at a level far below that authorized by Congress, it has had a substantial impact and has built firm and continuing collaboration in all states and territories.

Consequently, this recommendation is addressed, first, to administrative staff in institutions of higher learning and in alternate systems, since the Commission believes that inventive collaboration most often starts at the local level of service to the learner; second, it is directed to all those who support education financially at the policy-making level: Congress, legislatures, coordinating councils, boards of trustees, and bodies who sponsor alternate systems of education. In as large and complex a society as that of the United States, it is too much to hope that a completely coordinated and harmonious integration of services, free of gaps and duplication, can be achieved. But the creative blending of services and functions is a major positive step in expanding the availability of education.

35. *The techniques used by the Commission on the Accreditation of Service Experience* (CASE) *of the American Council on Education should be used in other alternate systems to establish credit and other equivalencies for courses offered by government, industry, and other sponsors.*

CASE was created in 1945 to evaluate military educational programs and provide collegiate registrars and other interested persons with the information necessary for granting credit for such programs. Schools operated by the armed services not only provide advanced technical competence but sometimes include components of general education. On request, CASE examines a service school and recommends whether its work is at a level such as to merit the awarding of credit and, if so, how much and of what sort.

Thus any officer who attended the National War College between 1956–1957 and 1967–1968 has, CASE believes, received instruction equivalent to "fifteen semester hours in political science, including international relations, nine semester hours in recent and contemporary history, and three semester hours in business administration" (Turner, 1968, p. 350). Such recommendations are issued periodically in guides issued by CASE and are widely accepted by institutions of higher learning. In a study of 1,968 colleges and universities in 1969, 1,097 reported they would grant credit on this basis, 407 said they would not, and the remaining 464 had no policy on the matter (*Newsletter. . . ,* 1969, p. 4)'.

In addition to assigning credit ratings to existing courses, CASE counsels designers of armed services programs who seek its help. The pattern of service developed by CASE seems capable of reaching out to all alternate systems which sponsor collegiate-level courses—in particular, industry, civilian government agencies, unions, and proprietary schools of all sorts. This new service would need initial subsidy, but eventually some form of payment, most probably fees paid by the organizations whose work is being evaluated, could make it self-supporting.

The Commission does not wish to prescribe details of structure and operation for this service. It suggests instead that the American Council on Education look into the matter, possibly through a broadly representative committee, and produce an organizational and operational plan. The Council might well consider two particular issues as part of this plan. First, while the semester- and quarter-hour credit system as we now know it is likely to continue to dominate higher education, some leaders of non-traditional education are adopting other methods of evaluation and record-keeping. These new methods should be incorporated into the equivalency system wherever possible along with the credit method. Second, many different alternate systems of education should have access to this service and could be involved in its planning. Present schisms and factions among them must be taken into account in developing the plans so that a unified and comprehensive equivalency structure can be evolved. It would be destructive of the whole enterprise for several uncoordinated ways of assessing equivalency to develop, each competing with the other.

36. The resources of communities and regions should be assessed to create an inventory of existing educational activities conducted by various agencies (business, industry, labor unions, and social, cultural, and collegiate sponsors) and thus identify the total potential of programs, facilities, and faculty.

Every community or region has within it a variety of training and educational activities that contribute in some way to the growth of the individual. All these should be catalogued in detail for ready reference and for future planning. An inventory of this type can be the basis for bilateral or multilateral efforts at non-traditional study; it is a tool for avoiding costly duplication of services within a specific geographical area; it is essential in providing generalized counseling assistance to the student; and it has great significance not only for financial economy but for better training and education. In fields where expensive equipment is needed for instruction, for example, the opportunity for academic institutions at the secondary level and above to use the workshops and laboratories of business and industry instead of installing their own can mean savings in capital outlay. It can also mean more up-to-date equipment and better instruction from experts in the field. Conversely, establishments wishing to have their employees develop their general education backgrounds or work toward higher degrees can find invaluable assistance and high-quality instruction in academic institutions and in various cultural agencies. Exploration of such overlapping goals on both sides could often lead to formal cooperative educational arrangements.

All these possibilities, and others not mentioned, begin with an inventory of resources. It is the first step toward considering and then acting upon an integrated concept of education in which the academic and community world merge their interests and needs. The current Five-County Project of the Syracuse University Research Corporation offers an example which may be useful elsewhere. Leadership in developing such an inventory might well be undertaken by public libraries with foundation or other support, possibly through the council proposed in the next recommendation.

37. A nationwide council, drawing together representatives of education and the public at large, should be created to build communication and develop creative coordination among the alternate systems of study and with the formal academic system.

No existing organization attempts to deal with the domain of out-of-school instruction in its entirety or even to conceptualize ways to deal with it. In fact, if the goal is diversity, a monolithic structure dominating this area would be fatal. Experimentation, freshness, and vitality are more likely to derive from a multiplicity of competing systems than from highly regulated institutional or organizational arrangements.

For several reasons, however, it is important to *visualize* the alternate educational system in its entirety. First, the goal of high-quality instruction for students at all levels and in all areas requires some mechanism such as an overall survey group for finding gaps or weaknesses and for stimulating corrective action. Second, some body or bodies should be charged with promulgating respectable standards to guide both producers and users of educational services. Third, organized sources of help are needed by community agencies which seek to inventory the several possibilities open to students in their region. Fourth, some representative body could assist in creating, operating, or monitoring services, such as a method for establishing credit equivalencies among alternate and academic systems (mentioned above in connection with the American Council on Education) or a national registry, as proposed in Recommendation 51. Fifth and finally, a broad, responsible nationwide organization of some sort should provide leadership for the whole complex of alternate enterprises, seeing that each receives suitable attention and publicity, stimulating the research and evaluation needed for their continuous improvement, and supporting close relationships between them and academic institutions.

The Commission thus looks upon such an educational council, perhaps requiring foundation support and resources from alternate systems, as both a liaison and a catalyst: a liaison among the diverse types of alternate educational activity, and a catalyst for stimulating collaboration between alternative systems and colleges and universities. It could dispel some fears of academic institutions that the competition of alternate enterprises will further aggravate their financial problems; indeed, it might even alleviate their burden by assisting other enterprises to take on certain aspects of training and education which they can perform better or more efficiently. Through collaboration and cooperation with formal systems it could help clear the air about who should give credit, grant degrees, guide students, provide materials, and recruit and make judgments on faculty; and it can provide guidelines for resolving such matters.

38. *Since public agencies have a special responsibility for coordination, educational agencies at all levels of government should coordinate their efforts more efficiently than at present.*

Government has become so complex that the task of effective coordination of service grows ever more difficult. However, the Commission has seen evidence of government interest in increasing the articulation of the academic and alternate systems. It is also cognizant of government efforts to reduce duplication and gaps in service in functional areas other than education. Both observations lead it to suggest ways public agencies could work together more efficiently at the task of non-traditional higher education.

At the federal level, responsibility is fixed and clear: it lies in the National Advisory Council on Extension and Continuing Education, created by Congress in 1965 and made up of representatives of major departments and other agencies and twelve public members appointed to rotating terms by the President. One of its tasks is to oversee expenditures allocated under Title I of the Higher Education Act of 1965. A second is to "review the administration and effectiveness of all federally supported extension and continuing education programs, including community service programs, make recommendations with respect thereto, and make annual reports . . . of its findings and recommendations to the Secretary [of Health, Education, and Welfare] and to the President." Until recently, the Council has not had its own staff and therefore has been unable to do very much to carry out its second function, but in 1971 it was finally able to launch a data-gathering effort to define its total task. This first canvass of the federal effort in adult education reveals a staggering number of programs, even though great caution was used in drawing the lines of inclusion. Excluded are such large and complex activities as the education of young people or the training given by the Department of Defense to military personnel and civilian employees. It was found that there were 143 programs in sixteen departments or other major units of government calling for a total federal expenditure of $4,091,597,000 in addition to the matching funds which must be provided by state and local governments or by universities. "This federal involvement," says the Council, "is massive, unorganized, and multi-purposed" (National Advisory Council, 1972, p. 12), as its report convincingly demonstrates. The Council has no illusions about its ability to change this situation immediately but it does propose a beginning plan to achieve greater coherence than before. The Commission on Non-Traditional Study wishes the Council well in its work and commends its report to the academic community, to high government officials, and to the Congress.

The responsibility for coordination at the state level is not so clear. To meet the requirements of Title I, every state and territory has set up a plan approved by the governor to coordinate academic and alternate systems by bringing together their representatives for the purpose of expending Title I funds. The state agencies which administer these plans may be the proper instruments to undertake

increased statewide efforts, and the National Advisory Council itself has recommended their use:

> Title I has created a working network for involving states,
> communities, and higher education in common efforts di-
> rected toward community problem-solving. This network is
> a valuable asset, not only for Title I, but as a vehicle
> through which other community-oriented programs of edu-
> cation, research and extension can be channeled. The major
> needs for the future are to use this network more broadly
> by channeling other related programs through it; to fund
> these programs at levels which will permit a substantial
> impact on objectives; and to give participating institutions
> assurances of long-term funding which will enable them to
> commit resources and develop programs having stability,
> permanence, and long-range objectives [1972, p. 96].

The Commission on Non-Traditional Study has neither the
data nor the experience to support the Council's suggestion through
formal endorsement, and it is also aware of how much the fifty
states and five outlying areas—all of which have coordinating units
—differ from one another. In some places another existing agency
may be better able to meet the need for coordination than the state
agency which administers Title I; elsewhere, the creation of a new
organization might be wise. The Commission is certain, however,
that governors, legislators, governing boards, and educators in many
kinds of institutions should recognize this need for coordination and
find ways to advance it.

At the local level, the problem of coordination is very complex and must be solved, if it is to be solved, in many different ways.
As suggested previously, the public library, which already provides
some coordination by trying to meet the resource needs of other
agencies, could take on other coordinating functions. Another possible community institution for this work is the local extension office
of the land-grant university, although retraining its workers to fulfill this function would be a major task. Still another institution,
which would have the same need for staff training, is the local
community college.

The wisest solution might be to create a new local council involving private as well as public agencies with a mixed lay and professional board and a paid staff to carry out its work. The local welfare council, particularly if it has a community referral service, would be a useful prototype for this kind of agency. Social service institutions long ago gave up the idea that each of them should be omnicompetent in meeting all community needs. Each defines its own task and concentrates on it. The citizen who needs help does not have to go on a dreary round of agencies trying to find one which will give the kind of specialized service which is needed. Instead, a central service has been created to help achieve this purpose. Such councils also carry out other functions: they train board members of agencies, train and place lay volunteers, plan and administer citywide meetings for both lay and professional audiences, bring new issues to the attention of decision-makers, and create a favorable climate for the advancement of social welfare in the community. Usually they are linked in some fashion with the Community Chest, which raises money chiefly from private sources to help support welfare efforts. If these tasks can be performed for welfare, they can be performed for education.

The Commission recommends therefore that at the local level, government authorities, and perhaps private agencies as well, try a number of different approaches. Pilot programs, each backed by local enthusiasm and using a structure and approach acceptable to the community, would reveal the strengths and weaknesses of each plan. Perhaps in time—and it may be a long time—a dominant local pattern of service to the citizen will emerge.

Alternate Technologies

The second set of recommendations on alternate approaches to education bears directly on the new technological tools developing so rapidly and already having great implications for reaching large numbers of students, offering independent study in a new dimension, and effecting financial economies.

So far, the long-heralded wedding of instructional technology and formal education has not come about for a variety of reasons, and both parties to the hoped-for ceremony are feeling frustrated. The material available through such new media as television and computer-assisted instruction has in many cases not been exciting educationally. Educators find the fast-moving developments of technology baffling and use their puzzlement as both a reason and an excuse for not making the capital investment needed to take advantage of what exists. Moreover, the tendency to shy away is strongly reinforced by the tradition of "each teacher supreme in her own classroom."

Technological development no longer seems to be the primary problem; the existing tools are ample and splendid, with more to come. The problems are rather of two sorts: institutional or organizational invention and coordination of program materials, and changing educator attitudes toward the use of the new tools and materials.

The Commission's comments on these issues stem largely from the data of its study of non-traditional programs, its discussion with various educational technologists, and position papers prepared by Frank W. Norwood, executive secretary of the Joint Council on Educational Telecommunications (JCET), and Wesley W. Walton of the Educational Testing Service (ETS). These comments also take account of the monograph published by the Carnegie Commission on Higher Education (1972a), the paper issued by the Commission on Instructional Technology (1971), and the report of the Sloan Commission on Cable Communications (1971). They therefore try to avoid repeating much of the information and recommendations contained therein except in areas where the present Commission adopts a somewhat different point of view. The Commission also calls attention to *The Field of Educational Technology: A Statement of Definition,* prepared by the Definition and Terminology Committee of the Association for Educational Communications and Technology (AECT) (1972), which describes in detail what is meant by the term *educational technology.*

39. Strong and systematic efforts should be made to reexamine the possibilities offered by educational technology and to improve and accelerate the adaptations necessary for its various uses.

This broad recommendation, as well as other recommendations in this section, is directed to the Joint Council on Educational

Telecommunications, the Corporation for Public Broadcasting, the National Association of Educational Broadcasters, the Interuniversity Communications Council, the AECT, the academic community at large, government, industry, and foundations interested in the exploration and development of electronic learning and information dissemination.

The major problems in educational technology may be divided into several specific components: the lag between engineering capability and social acceptance; the policies and techniques of management and production, including structural, collaborative, and legal necessities for swift and effective development; the economic unknowns that require research, together with those for start-up costs; the adaptation of teacher education to promote understanding and use of educational technology in appropriate and educationally strengthening ways; the means of effecting economies through the scale and critical mass of operation without creating centralized control.

The whole field is becoming so complicated and the choice of devices so broad that decisions to be made about future trends and priorities are difficult. Yet the potentials are breathtaking: possibilities for increased communication between learner and teacher; elimination of time-space constraints with videotapes and cassettes; breaching the restrictions of geographic distance by means of satellite broadcasting. But these and other possibilities are not easily achieved.

It is easy to be cynical about innovation in education; everyone recalls highly touted methods or systems which came to nothing or had very little influence. Cycles of rising enthusiasm, optimistic predictions, substantial investments, and disappointing results have become something of a pattern in the history of educational technology. Some might conclude that air conditioning in the lecture halls is a more realistic example of the true impact that technology will have on teaching than videotape, language laboratories, or computer-assisted instruction. But there are many examples of inventions that have been absorbed by educational systems, among them the use of xerography to reproduce textual materials, the development of long-playing records and audio cassettes, and the proliferation of paperback books. Still newer methods and systems need to

be examined and used by educators, even on an experimental basis
with some relaxation of traditional requirements, in order to discover the extent and quality of their effectiveness.

As yet these new methods have not been accepted very
widely in existing non-traditional programs. Of the 351 selected
programs analyzed by the Commission, data on instructional
methods were unavailable from 4 percent, but the figures in Table
12 indicate the extent to which various learning options are used.

Table 12

Use of Instructional Methods in
Non-traditional Programs

Method	Much use	Some use	No use
	Percent		
Traditional classroom lecture	38	41	17
Field work or cooperative work study	28	38	30
Tutorial	19	46	31
Programmed instruction	11	33	52
Tape cassette instruction	10	36	50
Occasional short-term campus residence	7	22	67
Correspondence	6	15	75
Closed-circuit TV or videotapes with no feedback	2	9	85
Closed-circuit live talk-back television	2	9	85
Broadcast radio or television	1	12	83
Computer-assisted instruction	1	6	89
Talk-back telephone instruction	14	6	76
Other	2	18	76

Not only is there little acceptance of electronic methods by
program planners, but desirability of new methodologies is not evident to would-be learners. In the Commission's survey of would-be

learners, all adults who said they would like to know more about some subject (78 percent of total studied) were asked: "How would you want to learn this area if you could do it any way you wanted?" The percentage of people responding to each method suggested is shown in Table 13.

Table 13

PREFERRED INSTRUCTIONAL METHOD OF WOULD-BE LEARNERS

	Percent
Lectures and classes	28
On-the-job training, internship	21
Short-term conferences, institutes, workshops	14
Individual lessons from a private teacher	8
Discussion groups, informal book club, or study group	7
Study on my own, no formal instruction	7
Work on a group-action project	3
Travel-study program	3
Correspondence course	3
Television or video cassette	1
Radio, records, or audio cassettes	1
Other	1

In view of the successes achieved by the new technologies in experimental programs where they have been used with skill and ingenuity, it seems clear from these data that important educational opportunities are being missed. Only part of the problem lies in the very high initial costs required for such programs and the vast numbers of students needed to make them economical on a unit basis. Those who believe that technology could make substantial contributions if only it were given the chance argue that faculty resistance, administrative indifference, and insufficient funding have prevented education from realizing the higher productivity at lower cost that technology has demonstrated in other areas of our national life.

One cause of this resistance and indifference is the widespread fear that technological methods of instruction will dehumanize the educational process. This view, if expounded by Mark Hopkins from one end of the log, might be more persuasive than it is when declaimed from the front of a one-thousand-seat lecture hall or pounded out on a professorial electric typewriter. Education can be a cold, mechanical, and impersonal process with or without technology, and though technology's record contains much that deserves condemnation and ways to improve that record are needed, depersonalization is not its inherent consequence.

The image technology presents is like that of industry in a Dickens novel. In no small measure this picture results from our tendency to use educational technology merely as a substitute for hand labor. Thus Edwin G. Cohen, executive director of the National Instructional Television Center, says with great accuracy that for more than twenty years we have talked about *instructional television* but have instead produced *televised instruction*. One can argue that a close-up view of a professor on a television screen is no less a depersonalized experience than a "long-shot" of him in real life from the balcony of a lecture hall. This argument notes that we have seldom used the medium to best advantage to make positive contributions to the learning process. While Chu and Schramm (1968), in their analysis of instructional television research, conclude that in the majority of cases no significant differences between classroom instruction and televised instruction could be discovered, one suspects that in the vast majority of cases the students were not exposed to significantly different forms of teaching.

A second fear—that technology will make of higher education a rigid, national, homogenized scheme of mass-produced curricula and students—has more foundation, although such a result is more likely to occur in the People's Republic of China than in this nation of educational diversity. Certainly it is not true that technology, to be efficiently used, must narrow our range of choices. Wisely applied, technology can be used to make available a new richness of resources, as the paperback—and, in fact, the invention of movable type—amply demonstrates. Technology is a response, appropriate or inappropriate, to a perceived need. If, on the university campus, we have not used technology to increase the options available to students, perhaps our lack of wisdom rather than technology is to blame. If we use technology during a period of mounting enrollments and shortage of qualified faculty merely to expand the walls of the conventional lecture hall, we should hardly be surprised that it has not magically fulfilled the individual needs of students. But if the university now gives priority to providing the student with a range of choices in determining the time, place, content, and style of his learning experience, then technology will be a means of avoiding homogenization and single-pattern mass production.

A third common assumption about technology is more evident from our actions than from our words. Much of what we have done in the past indicates a belief that technology is what one uses when one can't "do it right." The instructional film becomes the last refuge of the unprepared lecturer. Closed-circuit television is used when the freshman enrollment exceeds the capacity of the largest lecture hall on campus. Language laboratories are considered second-rate substitutes for individual tutorials. The image persists in the academic community of the professor helping his small band of students around the seminar table to wrestle with information and ideas. But as self-directed and self-motivated learning grows as an academic ideal, more attention can be given to the role which technology can play in offering more individualized, independent study rather than merely substituting for other methods. In this connection, various components of educational technology, if properly employed, can provide increased educational opportunities for people who are excluded from traditional educational patterns because of location, economic status, age, or family or business responsibilities.

More than likely, because of these prevailing attitudes, new areas of knowledge and course content will use technology more than older subjects which are constrained by a web of established practices and conventional wisdom concerning the "right" way to teach, just as extramural education rather than on-campus courses, as the Carnegie Commission notes, can be a particularly rich environment in which technology in education can develop. Efforts to provide educational experience at the postsecondary level for Appalachian communities or Alaskan villages (or even different

parts of a university's home city) are less likely than campus programs to meet resistance from an established faculty if only because
they do not threaten technological unemployment. Thus, while the
debate continues on campus, non-traditional studies and educational
technology may find themselves in a natural and mutually beneficial
partnership elsewhere.

On campus, traditional ways of teaching are currently under
siege. Students, faculty, administrators, and taxpayers are one in
their insistence that the old order with its senior professors filling
large lecture halls and its teaching assistants providing the major
human contact in the educational process must undergo substantial
modification. With the university's role as a teaching institution
being recognized as equal to or more important than the university's
function as a community for scholarship and research, it appears the
time is ripe to examine the spectrum of technology to find what, if
anything, it can offer to meet instructional needs on campus as well
as off.

A major step in this direction has been the recent establishment of a Center on Educational Technology in the Department of
Health, Education, and Welfare. The Center's first responsibility is
to "develop precise descriptions of educators' need with regard to
educational technology"—a task definition which reflects the oft-
heard question, "What steps should be taken to assure that the
benefits of instructional technology will be realized in an orderly
and reasonably prompt manner?" The Commission applauds this
development and urges further support for this Center.

*40. The potentialities of cable television should receive the
most careful scrutiny by educators and others interested in education; they should be identified, explored, and treated as speedily as
possible because they represent an important part of education's
future.*

In *The Fourth Revolution,* the Carnegie Commission correctly identifies cable television as an area of communications
growth worthy of the close attention of the educational community.
Like education, present-day communications are bounded by a
number of constraints likely to be greatly reduced by the introduction of new technology. One of the most significant facts about
cable television is that it is not bound by the severely limited num-

ber of channels for television and other communications which presently exist in any community. Thus the Sloan Commission on Cable Communications (1971) terms it "the television of abundance" and observes that it is "not merely an augmented television of scarcity . . . the analogy is not to conventional television, but to the printing press."

Television in the sixties and seventies resembles magazine publishing in the thirties and forties in that a limited number of media compete fiercely for the attention of a mass common-denominator audience. In the years following World War II, as television established itself, the mass magazines found that their declining revenues from advertising would not support their circulations. *Liberty,* the *Saturday Evening Post, Look,* and, most recently, *Life* passed from the scene, but their places on the newsstand and in the mailbox have been taken by a rich variety of more than forty thousand regularly published magazines, most seeking not the homogenized, middle-majority audience which read the *Saturday Evening Post* but specialized audiences, on the basis that every individual belongs to a dozen different special-interest minorities and that magazines depend on advertising aimed at their selective readers. The promise of multiple channels of television via cable is that video programming can come to resemble publishing more than it does present-day broadcasting. This is a strong example of "diversity by design."

Cable television began as community antenna television, bringing improved reception and additional conventional television stations to outlying towns, a service which is still its distinguishing characteristic. Leaders in the cable industry, however, recognize that public desire for further conventional programs is not without limit and that the future of the industry will depend on new services, including original programs, pay-TV channels, and educational and information services, all of which it can and eventually will deliver.

In comments before the Federal Communications Commission, the authoritative Electronics Industries Association has suggested that CATV's present rush to wire the nation may have implications which extend beyond the imagination of any present observer. It notes that a century ago the nation was wired for the first time for the immediate purpose of replacing the gaslight with the incandescent lamp. No observer then could have foreseen the multitude of services that would eventually be provided as the result of the electric outlet on the wall. Similarly, providing the American home with a broadband communications link to the outer world may prove in time to be equally significant in modifying our expectations and our life style.

Almost everyone agrees that cable communications can vastly increase the number of television channels available, allowing programs for minority interests to be delivered to the home and, because the cost of each opportunity to use the cable is low, to be repeated many times to fit better the schedule of the intended recipients. The most significant difference between cable and broadcast television, however, is that a cable connection to the home can carry signals from as well as to viewers.

Recent policy decisions by the Federal Communications Commission provide a favorable climate for this possibility: in the 100 larger metropolitan areas, new FCC rules require the eventual development of two-way cable communications. In addition, the FCC requires that one channel on CATV systems in major markets be made available without cost for educational use. In many other cities, the cable operator may be willing to do so on his own if excess channels are available and if such cooperation with educational interests does not place undue burdens on him. Further, the Supreme Court has upheld the FCC's right to require CATV systems to originate programming on the cable. Consequently, educational institutions interested in producing programs may find not only that they have access to the cable systems without charge but that they may, indeed, help the cable operator meet his own responsibility for making original, nonbroadcast programming available.

Such cooperative efforts should begin now. The FCC's designation of a cost-free channel for education is only for a five-year term, after which the policy will be reexamined on the record of experience. Thus, a prompt beginning, particularly in creating distinctively new and high-quality programs, will help assure continued and possibly expanded access for education to cable television.

41. Videotapes and cassettes should be carefully evaluated as devices for adding new dimensions of time, space, and flexibility to the learning process.

Important among the other technologies which will do much to reshape our current communications are video recordings or playback devices or both. Some years ago, "electronic video recording" (EVR) was announced with much blaring of trumpets. It promised a relatively inexpensive device which could be attached to any television set and which would scan recordings produced on 9.5mm film and translate them into television pictures in black and white or in full color on the home television set. In many ways, EVR was to be analogous to the long-playing record, an earlier child of the fertile brain of Peter Goldmark at the Columbia Broadcasting System. CBS's subsequent withdrawal from EVR and the equally embarrassing demise of RCA's laser-based Selectavision not only disillusioned many former true believers, but also tended to obscure the slower and less spectacular development of low-cost recording and playback devices based on conventional videotape technology.

Whether by the perfection and cost reduction of helical scan tape recording or by the emergence or reappearance of some new video playback technology, it is apparent that video cassettes or their relatives will play a role of increasing importance. Although formal education has not yet capitalized on the fact, videotape-based cassette systems appear to be enjoying a slow but healthy development. Courses in such varied subjects as *Ground Training for Private Pilots* and *Successful Salesmanship* are already available from proprietary schools.

Even more substantial is the amount of educational material available on audio cassette. The audio cassette has had wide acceptance as an in-the-home device: an hour's recording can be produced in quantity at very low cost, and battery-powered playback devices may be purchased for twenty dollars or less.

The significance of such devices is that they are "off-line, on-demand" systems. During the past twenty years, the development of instructional television in secondary and higher education has been blocked by the difficulty of fitting student and class schedules to broadcast television station schedules. While the multiple channels of CATV expand the opportunity to offer and repeat programs at convenient times throughout the day or week, video and audio cassettes can be individually available, checked out for use in library carrels or at home. Perhaps it is worth noting that the one piece of educational technology which has found acceptance—the book—is also an off-line, on-demand information device.

Beyond this potential of CATV to remove constraints on the number of available channels and that of cassette systems to remove time restrictions, they also lessen the constraints of being on a campus or in a classroom and following rigid schedules. The student may use them when and where he chooses. Any technology which promises such flexibility deserves consideration by those planning non-traditional educational systems.

42. Intensive study should be made of the long-range educational possibilities of satellite broadcasting.

A major inhibition of present use of communications is geographic distance. While electronic communications in various forms can span barriers of distance, ordinarily costs rise in proportion to distance. Now a new opportunity presents itself in the development of satellite communications. Their significance lies not in the satellite's ability to transmit to half the globe but rather in the fact that communication via satellite is insensitive to distance. In general, communications satellites operate by relaying information from one station on the earth to a satellite twenty-two thousand miles over the equator and back to one or more earth stations. The cost of such communication is the same whether the sending and receiving stations are located a block or a continent apart.

Among the most obvious implications for education of this fact is that educational resources which could never be delivered to rural areas at reasonable cost now fall within the range of possibility. In a few years, the government of India will conduct experiments using the National Aeronautics and Space Administration's Application Technology Satellite F to test the effectiveness of television programs designed to increase literacy, improve agricultural production, and provide information on family planning to five thousand village receiving sites. By and large, rural India has no terrestrial communications facilities. The construction of a conventional television network would not only be more expensive than transmission from satellite to special receivers of modest cost in village squares but, even if these expenses could be covered, the task of wiring up India for conventional television broadcasting could not be accomplished in fewer than twenty years.

Conventional wisdom about satellite communications tends to be based on the public's acquaintance with Comsat-Intelsat satellites, designed to serve as transoceanic links between existing sophisticated terrestrial systems. Economics and sound engineering practice dictate that such systems be designed to minimize satellite costs at the expense of requiring very large, complex, and costly ground installations. As NASA's ATS satellites demonstrate, such a configuration is not the only one possible in satellite communications. Satellites for educational purposes should serve a very large number of ground terminals as in the Indian experiment. In consequence, such systems need to invest heavily in the space segment and employ highly directional space antennas to concentrate all the available energy on the target area. Television reception can thus be provided, in some cases with return voice, digital, or video circuitry, to earth stations costing only a small fraction of what Intelsat satellites now cost.

That a satellite system designed for education's needs can bring communications at reasonable cost to remote areas is already being demonstrated in experiments via NASA's ATS-1 satellite, which brings health care information and instructional radio to native villages in rural Alaska. The earth terminals used in the villages are capable of two-way voice communications and are nothing more than modified taxicab radios. More sophisticated experiments are scheduled for ATS-F before it is repositioned for its Indian programs. ATS-F will provide instructional television services to the Rocky Mountain States, Appalachia, and Alaska by delivering television to schoolhouse rooftop antennas costing less than one thousand dollars each; and it can be used for two-way voice and computer communications. This technology, when combined with conventional ETV broadcasting or CATV, can provide televised instructional services to rural homes as well as to schools and community centers.

In a two-year study on Useful Applications of Earth-Oriented Satellites, the National Academy of Sciences (NAS) noted that communications satellites for education could be of great value even in nations where complex terrestrial communications facilities already exist. It observed that many small, specialized audiences are widely scattered throughout the United States but, if addressed collectively, would represent groups of substantial size. To note some examples, biophysicists, medieval scholars, and professors of comparative linguistics may be found on many campuses across the United States but seldom have the opportunity for conversation except at professional meetings. Electronic communications by terrestrial means require leasing facilities which span large geographic distances at considerable cost per mile. The satellite, with costs insensitive to distance, can provide a means for continuing communication among such groups.

Put in different terms, the NAS study makes clear that communications technology in general and satellites in particular free us from traditional geographic constraints and make it possible for us to organize enterprises which focus on a community of interests rather than on geographic proximity.

43. Institutions with common academic interests rather than geographic proximity should organize collaborative arrangements for developing instructional resources appropriate to the capabilities of educational technology.

In education, as elsewhere, technology imposes its own rules of economies of scale and critical mass. As colleges and universities have used television for instruction, the production of "software" has been analogous to raising home-grown vegetables in a cottage garden. Almost without exception, individual institutions are the producers of the product they consume. For example, the university's wish to retain its autonomy combined with limited resources means that conventional instruction ends up being reproduced: expensive production and recording equipment are used to transmit and preserve on videotape the same instructional methods and devices which are commonly used in the classroom. While in some circumstances this format may be the most appropriate, the economics of cottage-garden production often make it inevitable.

An accounting of the entire investment in instructional television by the higher education community would likely show a substantial total. If the national investment in facilities were added to a realistic estimate of the hours and skills of student volunteer crews, professorial "overtime," and other hidden costs, the investment would probably prove larger than campus accounting practices now reveal.

It seems clear that unless a certain magnitude of effort can be mounted, effective use of much technology is prohibitively expensive. The same realities apply to the printed book as to the television tape or the computer program. It is worth noting, however, that advances in technology tend to reduce substantially the thresholds of critical mass. Photocopying machines and high-speed duplicators make it possible to assemble and distribute "textbooks" uniquely designed for specific courses or specific classes. In the library field, the development of microfiche materials makes possible respectable libraries in institutions whose fiscal and physical resources are modest.

Any discussion of economies of scale raises the spectre that ultimate economic benefits can accrue only from projects of monolithic proportion. If it is inefficient for a thousand institutions each to develop its own video and computer materials for Physics I, and if institutional resources would be better invested by being pooled in the development of one hundred Physics I courses, would not a wiser investment be to produce ten such courses, or five, or—ultimately—a single standard course?

This spectre of mass uniformity is haunting enough that those who fear it insist, not without reason, that some safeguards assure alternatives. One safeguard common in federal programs is to distribute funds by formula grants which guarantee that institutions in each of the fifty states get a share of the pie. Very often this formula has the effect of guaranteeing that no institution will receive a large enough sum to do more than make marginal improvements.

If centralized control is rejected as leading inevitably to national curricula, national courses, or even a national campus, and if formula grants are dismissed as tending to dissipate federal investments into thin air, then some other approach must be found. One that has been suggested on a number of occasions, most recently by the Carnegie Commission on Higher Education, is the establishment of regional centers in instructional technology to serve traditional institutions of higher education—and non-traditional systems as well—within their area. In elementary and secondary education the federally supported Regional Laboratories represent a somewhat similar approach.

The very concept of regional centers, however, suggests that they will be distinguished from each other primarily by their geographic context.This concept seems outdated. Prior to the industrial age, when Father Juan Junipero Serra established his chain of missions along the California coast, he located them so that none would be more than a day's journey by horseback from its neighbors. In the industrial age, cities sprang up at locations convenient to power, raw materials, and transportation. Yet one distinguishing characteristic of our present period is the fact that we are no longer bound as were our grandfathers and even our fathers by the tyranny of geography. Hence it seems somehow anachronistic to suggest that a university which sends its students to spend a semester in Europe or in the Orient should depend for the development of instructional materials on an entity located in a neighboring city or state.

One example is the three regional instructional television libraries established in the early 1960s with funding under the National Defense Education Act. The initial assumption was that the two agencies in Boston, Massachusetts, and Lincoln, Nebraska, would devote themselves primarily to distributing those programs for elementary and secondary education which were uniquely suited to the curriculum and climate of New England and the Great Plains states. From New York, the National Instructional Television Library was supposed to serve the remainder of the nation. Experience soon demonstrated that truly regional educational needs are disappearing as rapidly as regional dialects and that the variation among educational programs within a multistate region is likely to be far greater than any observable difference between regions. Even more evident is the broad communality of interest which cuts across educational enterprises everywhere.

It might be argued that, despite such factors, the concept of regional centers offers the best bulwark against the dangers of over-centralization and that for this protection we should be willing to see a half-dozen technology centers each develop Introduction to Psychology for New Englanders, Psychology I for the South, and so on. Yet effective technology is so expensive that it is not inappropriate to recall the six million dollars required by the first year of Sesame Street for planning, testing, and program production. If the task of producing this series had been divided among three or four regional centers and each had been funded with two million or less, the result might have been that we would have done no more than add to instructional television's sad record of mediocrity.

Admittedly, regional centers are not inevitably parochial. Divisions of labor could reduce or even eliminate man's visible tendency to reinvent the wheel. But carried to an extreme, such division of labor suggests some supraregional authority to decide which regional center does what.

A more attractive solution stems from the realization that the technologies in which we are interested are not at all like the heavy industries of the nineteenth century. Singly and together their strength is that they free us from the bonds of geography. Precisely because of new communications technology we may now put aside the conditions which governed Padre Serra and look to the development of cooperative centers based on communities of interest rather than accidents of geography. MIT's closest intellectual neighbors may be its townmate Harvard and the distant CalTech. With low-cost communications via satellite dialogue with both institutions is readily possible and at much the same cost. Video and computer tapes can be shipped cheaply and quickly across the country. The difference between local and long-distance calls is a three-digit area code. New common carriers promise to make transcontinental computer conversations inexpensive and simple.

A system of technology centers based not on geography but on common interest can provide desired diversity and guard against centralized bureaucratic control. Besides being in harmony with the very nature of technology, such an approach also recognizes that faculty members' primary loyalties are to their disciplines. A microbiologist is likely to consider himself or herself, first, a microbiologist; second, a professor (tomorrow he may be a research scientist in government or industry); and only third, a member of a particular academic institution. In contrast to the demonstrated shortcomings of a regional approach to instructional television, there have been some successful experiences in discipline-based cooperation. The School Mathematics Study Group, the CHEM Study, and the AIBS Biological Sciences Curriculum Study have drawn together experts from across the nation to design and implement new curricula for elementary and secondary education.

The establishment of a users' and producers' cooperative is

worth exploring. Some universities, particularly the largest, may feel that they have enough resources themselves for self-sufficient development of video cassettes, audio-tutorial materials, computer software, and other technological desiderata with which to create an extended university. Other institutions are optimistic that "publishers" and the "learning industry" can quickly fill the gap with a proliferation of videotapes and computer programs from which faculty and students in the extended university may feed as from a buffet. But belief in institutional self-sufficiency can hold only if we are willing to pin our hopes on televised instruction and close our eyes to the contrast between the dismal record of the past and what can be accomplished by imaginative instructional television. And reliance on commercial sources alone seems naive to anyone aware of the disastrous course of the "learning industry" born in the 1960s by broadcasters out of textbook publishers.

Joint planning and cooperative action, initiated by participating institutions themselves, escape the serious dangers of federal or regional domination and at the same time provide every cooperating institution with a greater range of opportunities and a richer vein of resources than even the largest could achieve on its own. Candidates for such cooperation might include the Empire State College, the State University of Nebraska, Minnesota Metropolitan State College, the University of California, and the University of Maine, which has publicly declared that if it is to extend its services for that rural and poor state, it must follow the path of technology rather than the edifice complex which has nurtured branch campuses and community colleges in wealthier locales. This list is only meant to sketch the scope of such a consortium: some of these institutions might, upon examination, be uninterested, while others not on it might well join it. The way to begin would be an open meeting of all interested parties to explore all possibilities for cooperative action.

Such a program should not repeat the mistakes of the past. Other institutional councils have done no more than create a common market for the exchange of televised courses, only to discover that their faculties could hardly be less interested in programs produced elsewhere; attractive and effectively done videotapes from one institution primarily resulted in sending professors at the other institutions scurrying to their own studios to do the same. Neither is there much hope in a consortium based on the division of labor, assigning Empire State College to produce a freshman history course while the State University of Nebraska produces Science Survey I. Again, the interinstitutional, discipline-based activities which have revised the elementary and secondary school curricula with new math, new biology, and new chemistry suggest a better way to develop materials which are widely applicable and institutionally palatable.

Moreover, it would be a mistake to see the production of "courses" as the goal of such cooperative efforts. If they are true to their nature, extended universities will do more than export the pattern of three one hour meetings per week for fifteen weeks to new, off-campus locations. Under any circumstances, attempting to achieve unanimity among consortium members regarding the scope, content, and form of a freshman psychology course would be a thankless, pointless, and probably misdirected task. To shoehorn institutions into common molds while at the same time attempting to provide increased options for the student would be anomalous.

The ultimate motivating force for much of what the Commission proposes to accomplish is the academic faculty. Only through their understanding and action can the gap be closed between engineering capability and acceptance. Gaining such understanding and stimulating such action are fundamental to the future of educational technology. In Recommendation 22 the Commission advocates greater effort in gaining faculty acceptance of different instructional approaches. In the area of technology this effort should include workshops within single institutions or among several institutions to make not only faculty but administrators, students, and even trustees familiar with what exists and what lies in the offing. Such workshops should be extensive enough to give a solid basis for understanding the new world of communications and its significance for improving and expanding learning; they should be regular enough over a period of time to have real impact; and they should be offered expertly enough to engender enthusiasm for new possibilities rather than dismay at the complexities of the task. Recommendation 54 below suggests one means for conducting interinstitutional workshops of this type.

If faculty are to be persuaded to involve themselves, they should be compensated through released time or money or both so that they can give time and energy to a new and arduous task, and they should be appropriately and publicly recognized for the leadership they display in such efforts. These are not calculated ways to win them over; they are proper rewards for the performance of unusually difficult and valuable services.

Finally, the Commission urges prompt action toward setting in motion the machinery necessary to accelerate the use of educational technology. Central to this action should be the constant awareness that each of these tools of communication has its own distinctive characteristics and thus its own educational opportunities. When such characteristics are exploited to the fullest, great and productive change can frequently be the result. When they are employed merely to present outworn processes or to perpetuate bad instruction, they do not warrant the cost and effort necessary for their use. In educational technology, as in every other aspect of education, what the student learns is still primary.

In sum, the Commission has come away from its study of the proliferation and growth of alternate educational systems and new technologies with a conviction that both are developments to be welcomed rather than feared. Some alternate enterprises have already shown themselves to be equal in quality to formal education offerings and occasionally better. With appropriate monitoring and close relationships with colleges and universities they can become an even greater force for educational good than heretofore and an added set of possibilities for the student. Some technological advances offer great promise for expanding clientele, offering high-quality learning, and lowering costs per student. The Commission believes that both the systems and forms deserve close attention, encouragement, and assistance.

5

ASSESSING
ACCOMPLISHMENTS

In preparing the proposal for the research studies important to the Commission's task and the future tasks of others, K. Patricia Cross stated that "the concept of non-traditional studies raises some fundamental questions for and about educational accreditation. . . . For one thing, there is a growing recognition that concern with the process of education must be balanced by attention to the products of education. Secondly, there is recognition of the blurring of distinctions between educational institutions and other organizations that are moving within the educational realm. At present, we don't know the dimensions of the problems that non-traditional alternatives will create for accrediting agencies, nor do we know what problems the accrediting agencies will pose for non-traditional studies."

The Commission discussed extensively the possible effects on institutional accreditation and individual credentialing of non-traditional study. Measurement that leads to such accreditation and credentialing is an enormous problem, one that may well become one of education's major battlegrounds. The introduction of new elements such as an emphasis on competence and performance, the questions raised about grading systems and work experience, the completion of formal home or classroom work, or the limitations imposed by restrictions in time and space—these and other unconventional features which lie at the heart of non-traditional programs portend complications of a serious nature, both philosophically and practically.

Where the Commission stands on accreditation and credentialing has been touched on earlier. New, flexible attitudes toward accreditation must be adopted by the responsible agencies if they are to keep pace with what is required by the introduction of innovative and experimental programs. Similarly, changes are needed in the methods and substance of current credentialing practices, and some tools to measure student capability and accomplishment must be recast or replaced, as organizations engaged in constructing and administering tests are already well aware. These changes should not open the door to any dilution of quality but rather should guarantee its maintenance at a high level. A judicious balance between careful monitoring and encouragement and acceptance of adaptations that meet current needs is the best kind of educational contribution these agencies can make.

Although non-traditional study is posing some new difficulties both for voluntary accreditation and for state regulation of education, it is primarily accentuating long-standing issues. Historic inadequacies in state licensure, evaluation, and approval of institutions have been dramatized by the vogue for discount degrees, just as long-term weaknesses in accrediting standards have been brought sharply into focus by new institutions and programs that are achievement-oriented and structurally and procedurally deviant from past standards. Thus, non-traditional study may well be the instrument that stimulates solutions to these problems not only for new and unconventional programs but for traditional institutions as well.

The Commission believes that accreditation of non-traditional programs and institutions should be assumed by existing agencies rather than by newly created ones. This separate-agency issue, it now appears, will not become as troublesome as anticipated —by and large, existing agencies are preparing to evaluate non-traditional institutions, programs, and credentialing centers as they develop. However, a far more critical problem is appearing: the probability that existing agencies will adopt new standards for non-traditional study while retaining standards for conventional education which negate the new efforts. If this occurs, it may bring an end to the credibility of accreditation at large. Obviously, standards applied to organizations which merely examine and certify competence must be different from those for institutions offering direct instruction. For example, the New York Regents External Degree program or a similar credentialing arrangement cannot be evaluated on all the criteria that are valid for accrediting Empire State College or the University Without Walls. But accrediting agencies should apply identical criteria of effectiveness and efficiency to *every* educational program of the same sort, whether it be traditional or non-traditional, residential or external. New standards are needed to supplant the old, not just supplement them. If the new standards are only supplementary, the Commission has been told by JB Hefferlin (1972)', "they will prove too little and too late to save accreditation. They will merely whitewash its sepulcher."

To cause these developments and changes to take place systematically and rapidly, the Commision is convinced that various forms of assistance will have to be provided, some involving techniques for making change a more acceptable characteristic of the academic world and others involving new specialized structures to undertake particular types of change. The creation of these new structures, however, will not lessen in any way the current responsibilities of existing institutions; on the contrary, their creation should strengthen responsive and adaptive attitudes toward student needs, as well as influence and assist the movement toward guarantees of high quality.

Institutional Accreditation

The recommendations of the Commission relating to accreditation and credentialing deal with four areas of concern: the Commission's determination to protect non-traditional flexibility from being abused by a minority of individuals and institutions who try to make it an opportunity for personal profit rather than legitimate academic change and thus ignore appropriate standards; its interest in encouraging ways to expand the opportunities of young people and adults to earn an academic degree; its equal interest in deemphasizing the necessity for academic degrees of so many types and for so many people; and its eagerness to see changes in the ways and materials for measuring student potential and achievement.

The Commission is pleased to note that moves in all four areas are now in progress or being discussed and planned. But more speed is necessary, as is increased commitment and stronger and bolder action. Even the swiftest actions will be none too soon; otherwise, the concept of non-traditional study will have been debased or even destroyed before it has been fully and fairly tested.

44. Accrediting agencies should be governed by a philosophy and by policies which ensure adequate consideration of the public interest as well as member institutions or their professions.

Most commonly, *accreditation* in higher education refers to the process by which an agency or organization evaluates and periodically reevaluates a program of study or an institution and reports, generally in a published list of approved programs or institutions, that it meets certain prescribed standards or qualifications. In the eyes of many, accrediting agencies are inordinately occupied with serving their member institutions or professions through a process of internal judgments. If these agencies are to meet the needs of non-traditional study appropriately, they will have to consider another orientation to be equally important: their responsibility for serving the public.

Such a change will necessarily alter their primary function. Until now, for example, regional associations have considered the improvement of education within their institutions to be their major, and sometimes their only, obligation. Yet many presidents of these institutions, when queried by the Puffer Committee for the Federation of Regional Accrediting Commissions of Higher Education, indicated that they benefited more from their own self-studies stimulated by the associations than from the assistance of association visiting teams, consultants, standards, and guidelines. The Puffer

Committee concluded that the regional associations have not succeeded greatly in their goal of improving education at member institutions but have instead spent their time "making decisions about current accredited status of member institutions or determining whether or not applying institutions should be admitted to membership. The great bulk of the activity of the agencies is directed to the evaluation of curricula and to making judgments about institutional status" (Puffer and others, 1970, p. 262).

They, like other observers, recommend that the accrediting agencies pay more attention than before to the public's need for information. The chairman of the Study Commission on Accreditation of Selected Health Educational Programs, Arland Christ-Janer, says that "underlying all our concerns is the realization that accreditation must be conducted with primary concern for the welfare of the public" (Study Commission, 1972, p. vi). This fact is particularly true in the case of physicians, lawyers, the clergy, and the members of other established professions on which society confers special rights and privileges not granted to other people. Jerry Miller of the National Commission on Accrediting has found widespread consensus among people knowledgeable about accreditation that serving the public interest should be a primary function of accrediting agencies.

Of all the functions of accreditation, the most important for the American public is to ensure, as the North Central Association puts it, that students "will receive a fair education for their investment of time and money" and that benefactors, taxpayers, and society at large receive a fair return on their invested resources. Accrediting agencies must help identify institutions and programs deserving the time and money of students and benefactors; they must indicate, at least by implication, that others may lack this quality. When they fail in this function, government regulation on behalf of educational users and investors expands to meet the need.

45. *Accrediting agencies should reexamine their standards to see how they need to be changed to allow the diversity required by non-traditional study.*

From the data available to it, the Commission would have reason to believe that nobody supports this recommendation more strongly than the accrediting associations themselves. In the long run, however, strong differences of opinion about policy and its execution are certain to arise, and the Commission addresses this recommendation to these agencies and to the whole academic community in the hope that agencies will permit enough room for institutional innovation.

The belief that accrediting associations are bastions of conservatism which resist all efforts at change seems to be part of the folklore of higher education, but the Commission has not found it to be true. If there is conservatism, it appears, on the surface at least, to be justified in maintaining basic goals and values and to coexist with willingness to contemplate new means of achieving them. The Southern Association of Colleges and Schools has recently based a complete reformulation of one of its basic standards on the results of a major study of non-traditional practices in its member institutions. A special committee of the Federation of Regional Accrediting Commissions of Higher Education has developed guidelines for regional evaluation of non-traditional institutions and agencies. Other evidences of concern could be cited, but these are perhaps sufficient to indicate a trend toward a broader and more open approach than before—an approach which will hopefully be further advanced as distinguished lay citizens are appointed to the boards of accrediting bodies under a new policy that is just beginning to be implemented.

It is a cliche of accreditation, however, that the associations which fulfill this function tend to adopt the standards set by leading colleges and universities. The sense of innovation that characterizes general accreditation today probably resulted chiefly from the strongly expressed need for non-traditional study which followed the unrest of the late sixties. Therefore, if all institutions providing new programs are resolute in holding to both their ends and their means, they are likely to have a powerful influence on other institutions and to reinforce the movement of accrediting bodies toward non-traditional approaches.

This view is fairly general today among colleges and universities themselves. Only 10 percent of the 1,185 institutions responding to the Commission's survey of non-traditional offerings felt that accreditation holds back non-traditional study; it was only fifteenth in importance out of seventeen obstacles or problems confronting the non-traditional movement. And few of the leaders of non-traditional programs interviewed for the Commission indicated any concern about accreditation, while those who did seemed unprepared to knuckle under—as the following comment from one president suggests:

> We agreed from the start that we would play the accreditation game in the traditional way but that if it got in our way we would not fall over and play dead—nor would we modify anything that we thought was a fundamental principle simply because some accreditor said we had to change. If we had to, we would fight them, because we feel that the . . . Association should be held strictly to its own statements of what its function is: not to establish absolute criteria, but to determine that colleges are in fact doing what they say they will do. In fact we know that various accreditation teams operate on a prescriptive posture, but I would be prepared to go to court over the issue, except that I don't think it will be necessary.

All these observations about the small impediment accreditation poses to non-traditional study may, however, be too optimistic for two reasons. First, they assume that the theories of quality which lie behind present accrediting procedures are sound; and second, they do not take account of the attitudes of the innumerable special accrediting bodies which deal with special areas of content or with the professions.

So far as the first point is concerned, and to put complex matters far too briefly, the quality of a program or institution may be tested by determining whether it meets certain structural and operational standards, whether its graduates reach a required level of competence, or whether it has added sufficiently to students' abilities as measured by the difference between their capacity when they enter the program and when they end it. The first of these three measures is the one customarily followed in one fashion or another by accrediting agencies, despite the fact that research has shown that there is no necessary connection between certain standards—such as expenditures per student, proportion of Ph.D.s on the faculty, low faculty-student ratio, and a selective admissions policy—and the cognitive development of students. (See, for example, Astin, 1968.) It may well be that the recognition of this lack of relationship is one reason why accrediting associations have recently been so ready to accept non-traditional study. What difference does it make anyway?

The other two possible criteria pose major difficulties for accreditation. Achieved competence at the end of a program may be chiefly a product of the power of a college or university to attract able students. If so, its excellence is that of a conduit and the competence of its graduates can be fairly well predicted by the competence of its entrants. The value-added criterion is always subject to the question: What values? If an institution knows that it is going to be rated according to the measurable changes it can bring about from the time its students enter until the time they leave, it is likely to set its goals in terms of those changes, paying less heed than it should to their inherent value in the life of the individual or the society. The general accrediting associations are well aware of such problems and are now fundamentally reexamining their standards and procedures. The progress and quality of non-traditional programs will not be hampered—and will indeed be strengthened—by this initiative.

The second major issue involves the specialized accrediting associations, which, with few exceptions, have not yet been exposed to non-traditional study in any substantial way. Their work is very heavily guided by reliance on structural and operational standards; many of these are highly specific, and some of them seem to outsiders to be incapable of defense on any rational basis. More than that, some of the professional agencies—law being a notable example—have long been engaged in feuds with institutions which did not meet "accepted" standards. To such agencies, the idea of non-traditional study and particularly of the external degree is likely to appear to be the reemergence of an old enemy. Some years may yet elapse, however, before non-traditional study establishes a threatening foothold in the professions, and by then the general accrediting associations may have solved enough of their problems to be able to guide the specialized societies.

46. State legislatures which have not already done so should

enact legislation and set up administrative machinery aimed at
guaranteeing an acceptable level of quality in all institutions within
their jurisdictions.

"It cannot be said that most states exercise even the minimum degree of control for the maintenance of educational quality
among private degree-granting institutions," Robert Reid concludes
in his analysis of degree mills. "State laws chartering institutions of
higher education are not uniform and are actually quite lax in
controlling educational malpractice" (1959, pp. 62, 8). The situation has improved only slightly in the past thirteen years, but notice-
ably in several states within the past two years. The general situation will probably continue to improve slowly while local conditions
will remain variable: some states will impose strict regulations con-
sistently; others will continue to fail to enforce their existing regulations; and a few will maintain the view that citizens should not be
prohibited from making fools of themselves if they wish to do so by
purchasing whatever education and credentials they desire. And
federal regulation, despite its constitutional limitations, will probably increase as a result.

State interest in educational regulation seems cyclical: the
last two upsurges occurred in the 1920s and the 1950s, and another
may now be imminent. The statistics on state legislation and regulation are difficult to interpret historically because over the years students of the topic have used different definitions and criteria in their
analyses, but on two different measures—state chartering and licensure as one and periodic reevaluation and accreditation as the other
—regulations have tended to increase among the states.

The most recent survey of state statutes covering the organization of private colleges and universities (Williams, 1970) indicates
that twenty-three of the fifty states then regulated the creation of
nontax-supported institutions of higher education by specific legislation, while the other twenty-seven states chartered colleges and
universities under general statutes for establishing any nonprofit or
profit-making corporation or under various combination statutes.
Among the twenty-three, requirements for incorporation ranged
from eight full-time professors in Pennsylvania to fifty thousand
dollars' worth of real property in California and a half-million
dollars of capital in Michigan, New York, and elsewhere. Among
the entire fifty, filing fees were as low as Nevada's one dollar.

The majority of states appear to extend the degree-granting privilege to these institutions simply on incorporation, according to an analysis of the Williams data by Nancy Berve (1972) at the Education Commission of the States. Only a minority impose any additional requirement before institutions can award degrees, primarily that of obtaining the approval of the state education or higher education agency.

Every state practices accreditation as we have defined it—including publishing lists of approved programs and institutions and reevaluating them periodically—of professional programs in such fields as teacher preparation, legal education, and training in the health professions. But no commonality exists among the states in the terms they use to refer to this process: they may *accredit, approve, accept, certify, classify, license, recognize,* and *register.* Most frequently, state licensing boards in each field are assigned the authority to approve these programs, and often their approval is mandatory before graduates of the programs may be certified or licensed to practice the profession or sit for licensure examinations. Most of these boards either are authorized by statute or are permitted on their own decision to use the lists of nationally recognized accrediting agencies in their approval processes; many of them employ the same standards and guidelines as the national accrediting agencies; some send staff members along on these agencies' visiting teams to coordinate state and national action.

Some states also accredit colleges and universities at large. That is, after chartering an institution of higher education and licensing it to grant degrees, some states periodically reevaluate its operation and either reaccredit it or, if necessary, remove its license or occasionally its charter. Authorities differ on the number, but most of them appear to agree that some twenty-one states undertake institutional accreditation, as defined here to include periodic reevaluation, and that another eleven or twelve do not. Together with the rest that may in part do so, these eleven or twelve conduct some evaluation short of accreditation, such as requiring annual reports from institutions, assuring that their degrees meet minimum requirements, approving vocational courses for state and federal support, and visiting an institution whenever inspection seems warranted.

All in all, probably between five and ten states have expanded their accrediting functions in the past decade; if the trend toward statewide coordination of higher education is any indication, even more will do so in the 1970s, as an increasing number of state legislatures realize (as did the Florida legislature in 1971) that it is necessary "to protect the individual student from deceptive, fraudulent, or substandard education; protect the nonpublic institutions; and protect the citizens of Florida holding diplomas or degrees."

In 1953, Madeline Remmlein prepared model legislation for the National Committee on Fraudulent Schools and Colleges of the National Education Association's Association for Higher Education, but with no visible effect. Now, however, the time appears propitious for another effort. The U. S. Office of Education has given funds to the Education Commission of the States for a task force or advisory committee to draft model legislation for regulating degree-granting institutions. This project of ECS deserves endorsement and encouragement.

From the point of view of the Commission, the ECS model drafting will be most useful: (1) if it covers not only degree-granting "institutions" that provide instruction, as has most previous legislation, but also degree-granting *agencies* that do not offer programs of study as such; (2) if it involves not only education statutes but also consumer statutes so that consumer-protection agencies in the states emphasize educational deception and fraud with other consumer problems; (3) if it assures adequate representation of laymen in proportion to academics on education-regulating boards, (academically dominated groups should most properly serve in an advisory capacity to these boards); and (4) if ECS goes beyond the drafting of legislation to recommend operating policies and standards for the proposed agencies and thus insure that their criteria focus on educational quality.

Evaluating Students

47. New devices and techniques should be perfected to measure the outcomes of many types of non-traditional study and to assess the educative effect of work experience and community service.

As has already been demonstrated in Chapter Two, people undertake learning for many reasons. For some the act of participation, the personal sense of growth, or the newly won capacity to fulfill an interest or solve a problem is sufficient reward. But most people want credentials of some sort (whether or not they need them for any practical purpose) to show that they have taken part in an educational experience, even if it has no true evaluation associated with it but is merely evidence of a certain amount of chair-sitting at the proper times and places, for a prescribed duration. And employers, awarders and renewers of certificates and licenses, admitters to advanced status, and other guardians of rights and principles demand evidence of disciplined accomplishment.

Many people believe that present systems of certificates, diplomas, and degrees are inadequate or inappropriate to meet current needs. The Supreme Court of the United States, as mentioned earlier, has held that employers cannot enforce educational requirements or test results as a condition of employment unless they are specifically related to the work required of a job applicant. And a growing number of educators are convinced that new systems of evaluation and credentialing are required everywhere in education. Harold Howe II of the Ford Foundation states this view succinctly:

> I want to comment briefly on the close relationship between career education and the need for new systems of providing educational credentials. Today's inflexible and frequently discriminatory requirements of a diploma or a degree in order to be considered for a job make little sense. They are quite rightly being attacked in the courts. What we need are some new systems for finding out whether an individual has the specific attributes to perform a particular task and the adoption of these systems by both employers and school.
>
> The United States leads the world in its understanding and use of educational measurement. It is high time we turned our know-how in this field to an attack on the rigid credentialing arrangements we have inherited from the past and to the creation of tests and systems of guidance that will channel people of all ages into jobs for which they have ap-

titude and skill, regardless of whether acquired in school or through experience [Educational Testing Service, 1972, pp. 34–35].

In the case of non-traditional study as carried out by institutions of higher learning, a major step forward has been taken by the development of the College-Level Examination Program (CLEP) and other similar examinations. Of the 1,185 institutions responding to the Commission survey of their non-traditional practices, 64 percent allowed credit to be given for CLEP examinations, and substantial numbers accepted other forms of tests developed by independent agencies, government, the professions, or the institution itself.

The major problem concerning the certification of proficiency arises, however, when institutions accept work experience or community service for credit toward a degree without assurance that such service has had the ascribed educative effect. Little or no difficulty exists when the experience is planned for the purpose of learning, is supervised by competent instructors, and results are verified by other qualified people. After all, clinical experience in a hospital, practice teaching in a school, and field work in a social agency have long been accepted parts of American education. A substantial amount of other noncourse work is now being accepted for credit by American universities, perhaps as a result of the student activism of the late sixties, as the percentages from the 1,185 institutions in Table 14 reveal.

In most of the cases in which credit was granted without course work or examination, the student may have been in contact with faculty advisors who could make an estimate of the nature and caliber of his work experience and how well it fitted into his program of study. While it cannot be ascertained from the data whether the work was done for credit in terms of some previous plan or with some adequate faculty guidance, monitoring of both sorts was not out of the question, particularly if the student was in residence at the time.

Some colleges and universities, though not many, will also allow credit even when work was undertaken before students came to the campus and when no supervision would have been possible. In response to the question whether any of the following four kinds

Table 14

PERCENTAGE OF INSTITUTIONS GRANTING CREDIT FOR
NONCLASSROOM ACTIVITIES

	Percent
Cooperative work experience	35
Volunteer work in a community agency	28
A completed work (book, piece of sculpture, patent, and so forth)	17
Study abroad sponsored by groups other than educational institutions	16
Participation in local community theater, orchestra, or civic activity	14
Formal courses of instruction conducted by business, industry, or government agencies	14
Student body officer or active participant in institutional governance	10
Sensitivity training or encounter group experience	7
Classes at local free university or local experimental college	6
Unsupervised foreign travel	6
Other	8
No information or no such credit granted	28

of students "would ordinarily receive any credit for their work experience without having to take a special examination or test," the percentage of institutions which would grant credit in each case was as follows: 8 percent for "a twenty-five-year-old student with two years' teaching experience in the Peace Corps or VISTA"; 7 percent for "an older man with ten years' investment counseling experience"; 7 percent for "a sophomore who dropped out of another college after his freshman year and worked in a newspaper office for a year"; and 5 percent for "a middle-aged wife with five years' volunteer social work experience." The Commission believes that formal academic credit should be given for such life experiences and community service, but only if they fit into some significant comprehensive plan for learning and if their educative results can be evaluated.

These requirements are all too often ignored by those who demand credit for experience undirected by the desire to learn. A childhood spent on a farm is not a substitute for a degree in agronomy or entomology, and subsistence for many years in a city slum is not the equivalent of a degree in social work or urban sociology. Yet some people today argue that raw experience does not merely supplement but is the same thing as university education, a point of view which Cardinal Newman criticized as being held by those who believe that "learning is to be without exertion, without attention, without toil, without grounding, without advance, without finishing." Such an idea, he thought, was abhorrent to the very spirit of education; he observed that "seafaring men, for example, range from one end of the earth to the other; but the multiplicity of external objects which they have encountered forms no symmetrical and consistent picture upon their imagination; they have seen the tapestry of human life as it were on the wrong side, and it tells no story. . . . Nothing has a drift or relation; nothing has a promise or a history." In contrast, true enlargement "consists, not merely in the passive reception into the mind of a number of ideas hitherto unknown to it, but in the mind's energetic and simultaneous action upon and toward and among those new ideas, which are rushing in upon it. It is the action of a formative power, reducing to order and meaning the matter of our acquirements."

If this position is correct, ways must be found for measuring the effect of work experience on the individual's accomplishment of the goals of his educational program. The ingenuity of the educational evaluator, of which Howe spoke, will perhaps devise new forms of tests which can measure varied learning outcomes with a precision not previously achieved. In doing so, however, the evaluator will have to turn away from the traditionalism of the school-college-university setting to examine other areas of experience. For in the world outside the school, the assessment of the effect of experience on the individual has not only been studied deeply by theorists but also put into practice in systems which influence the lives of many adults. Assessing growth and merit is a central concern of public administration, the armed services, professional societies, business management, and universities themselves. Rating scales, rotating work systems, and examinations which admit individuals to the elite or specialized groups of professions are everywhere.

The Commission therefore suggests that some generalized testing agency such as the Educational Testing Service follow up this recommendation by analyzing the vast experience available outside the formal education system to discover ways of evaluating work or service that may be usefully applied to non-traditional study.

Such an effort will require not merely the talents of a theoretician of assessment but also the active and continuing collaboration of specialists whose work is far afield from traditional systems of schooling. The product may be no more than a manual of techniques but it may also go beyond that to some new system of assessment. Until the effort is made, nobody can forecast the specific outcome, but the general result should be the development of more effective ways than are now available to test the educative effects of life experience.

48. Systems of quality control should be built into the instructional and evaluative aspects of non-traditional study whenever possible.

The need for such control is particularly strong when heavy or total reliance is placed on one method of teaching or evaluation. In traditional systems, particularly those which lead to degrees, quality is often maintained by the separation of teaching and evaluation. In a sense, each checks the other. This division is more common outside the United States than in it, at least at the undergraduate level. Thus in England examinations are set and graded by separate committees, one of whose members may know a student but whose ultimate decision is collective and therefore not likely to be dominated by the viewpoint of one member. The idea of the external examiner is also common, particularly at the graduate level, where the student must satisfy some expert from another university of his right to receive a degree.

While separation of function is occasionally found in baccalaureate education in the United States, the quality of instruction here is likely to be maintained chiefly by summing up individual judgments of faculty members and administrators. That is, even though a student may have some experiences with low-quality instruction, some of them perhaps of his own cynical choosing, the quality of his education is to some extent assured by the number and variety of his instructors, each of whom (in carrying out the American credit-accumulation system) makes a separate judgment about him.

If the quality of non-traditional study is to be maintained, important safeguards must be built into it. Many such safeguards are available. A contract for study can be approved and its results attested by at least two different faculty members. The work done by a student for a mentor can be examined by some third party. Panels of visitors to the program can be appointed. Independent examiners or examinations can be used. Field locations and the work done in them can be inspected. Outside consultants can be brought in to examine the program in whole or in part. Student and faculty opinion can be solicited on a systematic basis. These are but a few of the techniques possible, but they suggest clearly that if the will to safeguard a program's quality exists, ways can be found to do so.

49. Degrees should sometimes be awarded wholly by examination if two conditions are met: the institution concerned is an established and reputable educational authority; and valid and reliable examinations are available to test the attainment of the degree's objectives.

To some people this recommendation may seem a drastic step, but even before the announcement of the Regents' External Degree in New York State certain evidence indicated that a trend toward degree-by-examination was developing. Twenty-six percent of the 1,185 institutions analyzed by the Commission allow their students to earn more than one year of credit by examination, although some course attendance is required in most of these institutions. A small number of them claim that they place no limit on credit—that it is theoretically possible to earn the undergraduate degree entirely by examinations. Further inquiry to find out what actually happens in these institutions revealed that while it was indeed possible for a student to secure a degree wholly by examination, it was highly improbable that any student would be able to do so. At least at some of these institutions, the option had never been utilized.

Since arrangements of this sort are theoretically available, it might be concluded that this recommendation of the Commission for degree-by-examination is well on the way to being implemented. Lest there be any misunderstanding, however, the Commission emphatically has in mind implementation in practice rather than theoretical possibilities. It believes that while only a relatively small number of people may seek their degree solely by examination, there are some who can be served in no other way, particularly those who live in remote areas, those who are housebound, and those who are confined in various therapeutic and correctional institutions. Such people deserve to have special help in programs designed for their needs.

The two stipulations in this recommendation require brief elaboration. If an established educational institution, such as a fully accredited college or university or a valid accrediting association, wishes to place its reputation behind a degree-by-examination, then questions about quality performance are likely to be answered affirmatively simply because of this reputation. The dangers of the diploma mill will be somewhat avoided, and the initial presumption that the degree can be accepted as valid will most likely prove correct. In applying this stipulation, a question of judgment can always be raised about whether an institution is, in truth, an established and reputable educational authority—but this question is perennial in education. The Commission is not disposed to suggest more directive guides but leaves to the good judgment of the educational community the decision as to whether a college or university has sufficient integrity so that its degrees, internal or external, can be accepted as having quality.

The second stipulation is likely to be more limiting than the first, at least for the time being. A degree, to mean something, ought to have a coherence which gives it unity. The University of London, to take but one foreign example, offers external degrees in many subjects and at many levels: the general B.A. in fifty-nine subjects; the general B.Sc. in eighteen subjects; specialized B.Sc. degrees in such subjects as engineering, economics, and sociology; the master of arts of philosophy; the Ph.D.; and degrees in medicine, surgery, and dental surgery. This dazzling array of opportunities is made possible because the external student takes the same examination as does the internal student, and in some fields of practice he can take that examination only in London. It is hardly likely that a comparable range will be offered externally in the United States in the near future, particularly because of the credit-accumulation plan which is used here. As soon as the range of valid and reliable examinations for a degree is available, however, there is no reason why it should not be offered.

50. The teaching and the award of degrees and other credentials should be done in most cases by the same institution; however, in exceptional cases, under conditions which are carefully controlled by quality standards, degrees should be awarded by non-teaching institutions which may or may not bear the formal name of "college" or "university."

In this recommendation a real issue is mixed with a semantic one, as has been the case since 1836, and the Commission believes it is time to separate the two: to take a stand on the real issue and to dispose of the semantic one. The real issue is whether a degree should ever be awarded by a non-teaching institution. The Commission believes that this option should be possible, and that such an institution should have the freedom to award the degree on one or more of the evaluative bases customarily used for the purpose: comprehensive or general examinations, course examinations, credits transferred from other places, CASE equivalents, or any other means already in existence or devised in the future. Any such institution should have an integrity guaranteed by the caliber of its sponsorship, a stable financing pattern, and a staff which is competent to define the degrees it wishes to offer, to counsel students, to handle records, to administer the program, and to carry out the collaborative arrangements with other institutions which might become necessary.

The Commission favors the creation of this pattern essentially because it believes that some way should be found to offer an additional opportunity to those millions of Americans who have had a partial college education but have never been able to complete it and who need to find some way of gaining recognition by the degree for the work they have done or that they might do, using the resources available to them.

The semantic issue has to do with whether the institution which awards the degree should necessarily be called a college or university. Until very recently, it has always been assumed that it must be. Up to 1900, the University of London was a government department, pure and simple, and had no teaching staff. In the United States, only one state education department has the right to a similar designation: The University of the State of New York, which has protected its standing as an institution of higher education by periodically awarding honorary degrees and now is awarding earned ones. If other institutions wish to follow this example, must they create fictitious names for themselves? The English have now answered this question in the negative by giving the National Council on Academic Awards the right to confer degrees; in fact, in time, the Council may well confer more of them than any other institution in the country.

The Commission feels that any reputable educational institution which wishes to confer degrees under carefully controlled quality standards but which does not now bear the name of university or college should not have to assume such a designation unless clear, local reasons exist for doing so. The Commission does not recommend, by and large, that non-teaching institutions award degrees, chiefly because it believes teaching and the award of degrees should most commonly occur under the same auspices and it would like to see existing colleges and universities take greater responsibility than at present for conferring the external degree. However, it does recommend to both the academic and the lay communities that barriers should not be raised which would hamper the awarding of degrees by reputable nonteaching institutions which wish to do so.

Implementing Recommendations

In various recommendations, the Commission has touched on the need for new agencies to provide assistance to the individual student or to various kinds of institutions. For example, its proposal in Recommendation 37 for a council that would bring alternate systems together represents an organizational move designed to help coordinate the development of these systems and provide liaison with academic institutions for the ultimate purpose of expanding opportunities available to students. Both students and the institutions need several other types of organizational assistance if they are to take best advantage of non-traditional study. The following recommendations relate to such matters.

51. A national educational registry should be established to evaluate a student's total educational accomplishment as measured by course credits, examinations, or other means, keep a continuing file to which items could be added, and offer advice on ways to complete a degree program.

The need for this registry has become evident to many people, though they have used various names to describe it, such as credit bank, educational record service, or educational evaluation center. American educational systems are relatively open, at least when contrasted with those of other countries, which tend to have a fixed number of places in colleges and universities for which there is great competition. In this country, people move in and out of college just as they do in other walks of life. Instruction is offered at many places and under countless auspices, both formal and informal. The course credit is still the unit of academic measurement, but it has been supplemented by many devices which provide equivalents.

The net result is that a very large number of adults make up the potential market for a degree. Census figures indicate that in 1971 some 11,782,000 adults twenty-five years of age or over had had some college work but had not secured a first degree. If present provisions for education continue, their number will reach 22,305,-000 by 1990. In 1971, there were 38,029,000 persons who had not gone beyond high school completion and another 18,601,000 who had gone to high school but did not graduate. By 1990, these figures will have increased to 58,965,000 and 21,768,000, respectively.

Only a fraction of these people will secure a degree or want to do so, but there is evidence that the percentage is larger than most skeptics believe it to be. Respondents to the Commission's survey of educational demand were asked what educational degrees they would like to earn in the next ten years. Sixteen percent said they would like to get high school diploma, 8.9 percent desired a two-year degree, 12.4 percent wanted a bachelor's degree, 8.0 percent hoped for a master's degree, and 4.4 percent sought a doctorate of one kind or another. Though these figures do not represent the actual "market" for degrees, they certainly indicate interest in working toward them.

Various recommendations in this report suggest ways to meet the need for a degree, but they may not take care of the special situation of a large number of Americans who find themselves with many evidences of formal learning but with no institution available which will help fit them into a coherent pattern for a degree. The United States Association of Evening College Students recently issued a report entitled "Transfer of College Credits and Off-Campus Learning" (Meloni, 1972), which details graphically the problems these students encounter and suggests various solutions.

The Commission suggests a feasibility study to develop a detailed plan for the registry. The general outline, however, can be sketched in broad terms. The registry might be concerned, initially at least, only with undergraduate degrees. Its first function would be to build a record for an individual that would collect all relevant evidence of formal learning. Such a person would provide the registry with a list of colleges attended, CLEP or other similar examinations passed, proof of study in alternate educational systems, CASE or other equivalency records, and a narrative account of his major areas of life experience which might be eligible for college credit. It should be understood that such a record would be confidential and all steps necessary would be taken to keep it so. As new forms of evaluation become available, they could be added to the record, and the registry might play an important role in helping to stimulate such new forms.

The second function of the registry would be to counsel the student about any matters related to enlarging his stock of credits or other evidence of academic attainment. He might be guided to take courses or examinations or to submit evidence of experience to institutions which would assign credit for them. Aptitude testing might also be suggested.

The third function would be to help the student build a

program for the future. The existing record might fall into a coherent pattern which could be certified without further study. More
often, perhaps, several fragmentary patterns would emerge, each of
which would need to be rounded out into a coherent whole. At this
point, the extent and nature of the availability of external degrees become pertinent; some would be well suited for a particular student
and others would not. The best course of action for the student might
be to enter a traditional rather than a non-traditional program because of its geographic closeness, its nature, or even the sympathetic
understanding of its officials in dealing with unusual cases. Whatever the situation, the student would be helped to see the options
which lay ahead. At this point, some exploration might be required,
and various institutions could be supplied, at the student's request,
with the cumulative record which had been compiled.

The fourth function of the registry would be to maintain a
continuing record of the student's further educational attainments.
Some students might not require this service but would rely henceforth on the institution at which they plan to secure their degree. In
a sense, they would close their accounts at the registry. Other individuals might prefer to explore further before deciding finally on a
program. Or perhaps they would like the safeguard of a central
national record of their educational achievements. The registry
would then serve as a kind of bank in which the student deposits
educational credit. Since conditions of employment often require
people to transfer periodically from one community to another, an
individual uncertain about his eventual wishes for a degree might
feel the need to keep a cumulative record of his study in some
convenient place. The mere fact of continuity might itself be a
motivating factor for further study.

52. *A group of organizations (operational in character),
concerned about the future of education generally and non-traditional approaches in particular, should join in a continuing enterprise to examine and evaluate educational trends as well as encourage new possibilities.*

One of education's weaknesses today is its fragmentation.
Much good work is being done in specific and sometimes specialized
areas, but there is little indication of a master strategy based on a
broad overview of the field. Educational renewal and deeper in-

sights into the learning process are being called for as never before. To answer such a call creatively and effectively requires the examination of education as a total human experience rather than as an aggregation of disparate segments.

The Commission is convinced that a continuing overview of current learning theories and practices is an essential element in creating a strong educational process. Information must be generally disseminated on what is happening or being planned; appropriate and nonduplicative research should be undertaken; and experimentation must be encouraged. Above all, there must be identification of what is needed, leadership to move boldly on problems as they emerge, and recommendations of concrete actions that shape public and private policy.

No single organization or college or university can probably perform such a function, not even the nationwide educational council proposed in Recommendation 37 above. Nor is it likely or even desirable that a government agency can or should undertake the whole task. Any one of these has its own vested interest; each looks at education from a particularized point of view. What is needed is an amalgam of major organizations, each directly involved in major aspects of educational growth and progress: an informal consortium of organizations designed to look ahead at the same time it examines the present, possibly through periodic meetings of continuing representatives. This assembly should be able to move readily from theoretical considerations to a concentration on action, calling on individual agencies, institutions, and foundations to take on discrete parts of its task of keeping education adaptive to social needs and sensitive to its constantly altering circumstances.

The key to the success of such an informal assemblage lies in its ability to have within itself or at hand certain capabilities and basic tools: philosophical, in order to put educational ideals and practical goals into perspective; analytical, in order to scrutinize programs and trends, evaluate their significance and soundness, devise suitable measurement techniques, and encourage research; disseminative, in order to make certain that the academic world and the public are regularly apprised of what is happening and what it means; and catalytic, in order to stimulate program development, in-service growth of faculty and administrators, and foundation or government support.

The three recommendations that follow are, in fact, examples of the specifics that such an assembly should be expected to promote. They are not all-inclusive, but they are major steps toward strengthening the potential of non-traditional study. In each instance the consortium of organizations might create a small task force to plan and in some cases operate the specific enterprise.

53. A clearinghouse of information should be established so that knowledge of inventive efforts can be easily disseminated both on a regular basis and in filling individual requests.

A vast and diverse array of knowledge about non-traditional education is coming into being. The Commission, for example, has accumulated a considerable amount of such material, as have such individuals as John Valley of Educational Testing Service, Frances DeLisle of Michigan State University, and the researchers listed in Appendix B. An important necessity now is that this information be gathered systematically on a national scale and made easily available. The demand for such information will grow steadily and will come largely from individual colleges or universities, guidance counselors, libraries, and research scholars.

So far, several collections in various locations are duplicative and partial. The Commission urges, therefore, that at least one repository of material be created as an active library, that the academic world be made aware of its existence and services, and that additional information be channeled into it. Two possibilities exist for creating a repository of this sort: expansion of the responsibilities at one of the locations of current materials or organization of a totally new center.

54. A pattern of workshops should be created, particularly during the next three years, designed to make faculties, trustees, administrators, and student leaders familiar with non-traditional possibilities.

There is little doubt that current interest in non-traditional education will lead to a demand for inservice education and training so that college and university policy-makers can base future planning on a sound background of knowledge. Individual institutions have already organized conferences on their own campuses or created committees to look into such matters; national meetings of leading educational organizations have similarly held sessions entirely devoted to non-traditional study in general or to the external degree in particular.

These meetings have been valuable to institutions and individuals, but they now need to be intensified, made more specific, and arranged on a regular and more frequent basis. Such organizations as the Aspen Institute of Humanistic Studies in Colorado or the Educational Testing Service in New Jersey, which has just completed its Chauncey Conference Center, are typical of those which could develop workshop series. Continuing education centers on university campuses around the country also have such capabilities and might develop regional service networks. Most important, of course, is assurance that the workshops are appropriately organized and staffed for instruction and that there is continuity in their development from year to year. The assembly of organizations proposed in Recommendation 52 might sponsor or advise them. Such sponsorship would be helpful in assuring their quality and growth.

55. An Educational Curriculum and Research Service (ECRS) should be established to provide coordinated research, development, and service bearing on needs of individuals and institutions engaged in non-traditional educational activities.

The Commission regards ECRS as a support to academic institutions and other agencies involved in non-traditional study. Its essential characteristic should be professional competence, accompanied by willingness, even eagerness, to seek out and use the talents and capacities of others—faculty, librarians, researchers, publishers, specialists from business organizations, and the like. Its organization and operation should reflect this point of view by keeping its permanent staff small while developing a system for using external professional resources to meet the work load.

The Commission's subcommittee on Means for Non-Traditional Study specified a set of tasks for ECRS such as the following: carry out studies and surveys to determine societal, business, and personal needs for specific non-traditional curricula; provide the organization and means to modify existing curricula, coordinate the development of non-traditional curricula and new instructional support and delivery methods, and apply pressure needed to keep a variety of delivery options open; develop guidelines for evaluating student performance and achievement; prepare descriptive materials for use in explaining specific curricula to prospective students, participating institutions, and others; develop a communications network to keep institutions, publishers, and other companies informed about the specific instructional materials needed for a particular curriculum; and carry out research and studies to determine which curricula should be developed, in what order of priority, and the relative effectiveness of instructional methods for a given curriculum and a given type of student.

The two final recommendations, relating to assistance of institutions and of non-traditional study generally, need very little explanation.

56. The newly formed Fund for the Improvement of Post-secondary Education, created under the 1972 Amendments to the Higher Education Act of 1965, should assign resources for further development and encouragement of non-traditional possibilities of the sort identified by the Commission.

This new legislation, as quoted in the Preface of this report, clearly indicates the deep interest of the federal government in the possibilities of non-traditional modes and fields of study. The Commission calls attention to this fact in the hope that such interest and statements of intent will be followed by adequate appropriation of funds which the new agency can use to encourage educational innovation.

57. A conference should be convened in 1975, calling together those individuals, institutions, and organizations originally assembled by the Commission in 1973 to discuss its recommendations and respond to them. Such a follow-up conference should identify the nature of any action that has taken place, assess its effectiveness, and determine what significant progress non-traditional study has made during the intervening two years.

Remembering its determination to press for action wherever and whenever possible, the Commission urges that this same stimulus be maintained long after the Commission ends its formal responsibilities in February 1973. The suggestion of a follow-up conference in 1975 is an effort to keep educational decision-makers and doers aware that regular assessments of progress are important.

The new agencies proposed in this chapter and elsewhere

might be consolidated into a single structure, a national university, which would not only carry out all of their functions but would also, if necessary, award degrees itself. Such an institution was proposed in June 1970 by Jack Arbolino of the College Entrance Examination Board and John Valley of the Educational Testing Service. It was their suggestion which stimulated the two organizations to create this Commission and secure support for it from the Carnegie Corporation of New York. A summary of the Arbolino-Valley Report is presented in Appendix A.

The idea of a national university should be put into its proper historical perspective. Such an institution was first conceived in colonial days and was close to the heart of George Washington both as president and as a private citizen, for he left a substantial portion of his estate as endowment for the purpose. The first widely known detailed plan for a University of the United States was proposed by Dr. Benjamin Rush in 1787 and the idea has been recurrent ever since, but Congress was never willing to establish the new institution. Thomas Jefferson thought he knew why: "A 40 years' experience of popular assemblies has taught me," he observed, "that you must give them time for every step you take. If too hard pushed, they balk, and the machine retrogrades." As for the people themselves, Jefferson said, they "generally have more feeling for canals and roads than education."*

However unsuccessful the idea, both then and later, it has spurred change. The hindsight of the modern reader discerns in its various versions the nature of later reforms in higher education. Thus a plan put forward in 1870 by John W. Hoyt and introduced into Congress on his behalf called for the creation of an institution which could rise above existing institutions by offering a broad curriculum which included practical subjects, graduate study and research at the highest level, and the incorporation of professional education into the program of studies. These were precisely the major trends which were to occur in American higher education during the next fifty years.

---

* Quoted in D. Madsen, *The National University; Enduring Dream of the USA* (Detroit: Wayne State University Press, 1966, p. 49). All the factual information on the history of the idea of a national university is drawn from this book.

After long discussion, the Commission on Non-Traditional Study has finally declined to recommend a national university as a structural concept to embody its own proposed reforms. Opinion on the matter was by no means unanimous, for five Commission members did vote to recommend the creation of a new University of the United States. However, the majority believed that even though the Commission does not recommend that its proposals be implemented by a single new national entity, the ultimate effect will be the same as before. The Commission hopes it has discerned at least some of the diverse designs of the future which will be worked out (as history shows they always have been) by existing colleges and universities and by the creation of new institutions which fill in the gaps of service but seek no supremacy for themselves in the entire educational system.

A

SUMMARY OF PROPOSAL FOR A NATIONAL UNIVERSITY: MINORITY VIEW

Early in 1970 the joint officers of the College Entrance Examination Board and the Educational Testing Service asked Jack Arbolino and John Valley to prepare a plan for the study of the promise and the problems of an external degree. As part of their report, Arbolino and Valley developed the model of the National University. Their proposal is summarized below.

145

A National University should be established. As envisioned, it would:

(1) Award degrees, based solely on examinations, in its own name.

(2) Jointly award degrees with Participating Colleges. These would be degrees in which the majority of the requirements would be met by National University credits—credits earned by examination or by the procedure approved under function No. 3 below. The degrees would be awarded by the joint action of the National University and the Participating College. In addition, the Participating College would continue to award degrees in the traditional way as well.

(3) Accredit college-level instruction offered outside the colleges and universities. (The authors of the plan regard this proposed function of the National University as an important and original contribution.) This function is designed to make it possible for individual achievement to be recognized. It would not entail the accreditation of the agency offering the instruction but would focus on the adequacy of the particular instruction under question. One objective of this procedure is to make it possible for college-level achievement to be recognized without invariably resorting to the technique of validating examinations. Among the forms of instruction to be considered under this function would be correspondence, radio, television, and those forms provided by government, industry, business, the military, social services, and foreign agencies.

(4) Award credits and certificates on the basis of programs such as the Advanced Placement Program, the College-Level Examination Program, and the New York College Proficiency Examination Program, as well as on the basis of demonstrated achievement in professional and subprofessional fields.

(5) Help students who wish to transfer.

(6) Encourage the development of all instructional resources. (It should be explicit that the National University itself will not provide instruction.)

(7) Maintain records of individual educational accomplishment.

(8) Provide an educational counseling and referral service for individuals.

(9) Provide an advisory and consulting service on education for employers.

(10) Maintain a program of research and development supportive of continuing education.

(11) Provide the examinations and the other instruments and services necessary to implement the National University.

(12) Maintain an active forum including publications devoted to the development of continuing education.

B

RESEARCH
PROGRAM

The Commission's research program was undertaken by Educational Testing Service in response to the need for more complete and accurate data than were currently available. Its aim, beyond providing basic information for the Commission to use in developing its recommendations, was to present careful analyses and interpretations of current and evolving conditions related to non-traditional study to the profession and public at large. An extensive series of publications on the research findings is planned, to be issued after the Commission's own report.

A detailed proposal for the research program was developed by ETS in January 1971 and submitted to the Carnegie Corporation of New York and the Educational Foundation of America, which granted a total of $219,000 to ETS for this work. Codirectors of the research program were K. Patricia Cross and John R. Valley.

Wesley W. Walton served as program manager. The advisory council for the research program consisted of Samuel B. Gould, Samuel J. Messick, Robert J. Solomon, and William W. Turnbull. Cyril O. Houle served as senior consultant to the research team members.

ETS arranged through formal agreements with the Center for Research and Development in Higher Education at the University of California, Berkeley, the College Entrance Examination Board, and the Response Analysis Corporation to carry out or assist with portions of the research program. The research team was drawn from ETS offices in Berkeley, Durham, and Princeton, and from these cooperating organizations.

The principal means of data-gathering were (1) a questionnaire survey of a national probability sample of adults on their educational interests and experiences, by ETS and the Response Analysis Corporation; (2) a questionnnaire survey of opportunities for non-traditional study at colleges and universities, by the Center for Research and Development in Higher Education; (3) in-depth interviews with leaders of non-traditional education, by the Center for Research and Development in Higher Education; (4) in-depth interviews with experts in the knowledge and communications industries, by the College Entrance Examination Board; and (5) extensive reviews of the literature, by ETS.

In the first phase of the research program, the following three monographs presenting the new data from these surveys and basic interpretations of their findings were prepared:

(1) "Non-Traditional Programs and Opportunities in American Colleges and Universities, 1972," Janet Ruyle, JB Hefferlin, Lucy Ann Geiselman, Ann Kirton, Center for Research and Development in Higher Education.

(2) "Learning Interests and Experiences of Adult Americans," Abraham Carp, Richard E. Peterson, Pamela Roelfs, ETS–Berkeley.

(3) "Non-Traditional Study: A Critical Review of the Literature," William A. Mahler, ETS–Princeton.

In the second phase of the research, major areas of concern were examined by drawing on the information gathered during the first phase. Extensive "state-of-the-art" monographs were the result:

(1) "Non-Traditional Education: Opportunities and Pro-

grams in Traditional Colleges and Universities, 1972," Janet Ruyle, Lucy Ann Geiselman, JB Lon Hefferlin, Center for Research and Development in Higher Education.

(2) "New Paths for Adult Learning: Systems for Delivery of Instruction in Non-Traditional Programs of Study," Wesley W. Walton, ETS–Princeton.

(3) "Credit and Measurement in Non-Traditional Study," Jonathan R. Warren, ETS–Berkeley.

(4) "Cut-Rate Credits and Discount Degrees: Quality Controls of Non-Traditional Study Through State Regulation and Voluntary Accreditation," JB Lon Hefferlin, Center for Research and Development in Higher Education.

Although not expected as an outcome at the time the research program was mounted, the wealth of new and well-organized information on non-traditional studies has stimulated interest in further study. As the research program drew to a close several book-sized manuscripts were in the design stage and a prospectus on each was in the process of being completed.

C

FINANCING THE
EXTERNAL DEGREE

Howard R. Bowen

The term *non-traditional study* as usually conceived includes almost anything in higher education that is new, unusual, or not widely practiced—unconventional modes of instruction, such as independent study, home study, study aided by TV or computers, or study conducted in the community through internships or social service; non-traditional students, such as housewives, men and women in midcareer, the elderly, shut-ins, or inmates of penal institutions; unusual schedules, such as part-time study, work-study, shortened programs, or flexible programs. Un-

This appendix appears, in altered form, in the *Journal of Higher Education,* June 1973. It is based on a paper delivered at the 1973 annual meeting of the AAHE.

orthodox settings or sources of learning are increasing in importance
—the armed services, libraries, hospitals, proprietary schools, employers, unions, churches, government bureaus, museums, and
private tutors. Credit or degrees may be awarded by universities or
other institutions for study or accomplishments not conducted
under the auspices of the degree-granting institutions. Non-traditional study may also include job training, instruction in hobbies,
consumer education, and other types of learning which do not lead
to credits or degrees.

The many aspects of non-traditional study may be combined in different ways to form varied systems of instruction and
recognition of learning. One device for organizing them is the
external degree, a degree granted by a college or university, or other
institution, on the basis of learning acquired partly, mainly, or
wholly outside the walls of the degree-granting institution. In recent
years, the external degree has evoked considerable interest; several
institutions are already awarding it, and many are planning to do so.

In order to discuss the financing of external degree programs
one must specify just what kind of program one is talking about.
The model I have selected is one which appeals to me as representing good education. It is a model that I would be willing to recommend to my own institution or to my own son. I must confess, however, to some concern about the maintenance of quality and rigor in
external degree programs. I believe special efforts will be needed to
avoid erosion of quality as off-campus learning becomes a major
factor in the preparation for degrees.

The Model

The model contains the following features: (1) A well-
established college or university with ten thousand resident undergraduate students and seven hundred faculty members awards the
B.A. as its only external degree. (2) Students are recruited for the
external college program by appropriate means and are admitted
to the program by a formal procedure whose standards are comparable to those for other freshmen or transfer students. (3) At the
time of admission, each student's educational history and status are
carefully evaluated and a plan of study or "contract" for completion of the degree requirements is established. (In some cases, the

requirements for the degree would have been completed before admission.) (4) Learning from any source, both before and after admission, will be evaluated. However, students are encouraged when feasible to take the equivalent of at least one year of study through on-campus instruction at recognized colleges or universities. The purpose of this provision is to assist in measuring performance and to encourage at least some residence in an academic atmosphere. (5) No specific courses or subjects are required, but the total educational program must be appropriate for a degree signifying liberal learning and must have coherence. It must be more than a miscellaneous and unstructured collection of bits and pieces. (6) The academic standards are so far as possible comparable to those applied to resident students. Resident students have access to the same contract system if they wish and the same option of earning part or all of their credits through various forms of independent study and life experience. (7) The institution provides guidance and counseling to external degree students prior to their admission and during their progress toward the degree. It keeps in touch with students periodically and arranges campus visits for them when practicable. (Preferably, it serves students who live near enough to visit the campus for night or weekend courses and for counseling.) (8) The institution offers instruction to external degree students (and others as well) in most of the courses in its entire curriculum through the following modes: regular resident classes—all available to qualified part-time students; night and weekend classes or sections of classes—available to both resident and external degree students; independent study based on syllabi prepared by professors and including readings, exercises, papers, examinations, and so on, comparable to those in resident courses; courses designed especially for external degree students (but available to regular students) delivered by radio, TV, cassettes, computers, detailed syllabi, or other methods. (9) Preparation of courses for the external degree program and the work involved in conducting such courses become a regular part of the faculty work load. Hence the size of the faculty must be increased to accommodate the external degree program except when the program involves offsetting economies. (10) The hypothetical institution attracts, beyond its regular enrollment, four thousand external degree students (mostly part-time), or one thousand full-time equivalents, and grants four hundred external degrees a year. To maintain this number of active external degree students, on the assumption of a substantial dropout rate, it admits two thousand new students each year. Regular students account for two thousand course registrations in the external degree program and external degree students account for one thousand course registrations in regular courses.

Cost

Having described an external degree program in some detail, one can begin to estimate its cost. The following are my rough guesses as to the annual cost of this particular model.

Student Recruitment. To recruit the two thousand students a year needed to maintain an enrollment of four thousand would require advertising and public relations expenses as well as personal interviewing and correspondence. The annual cost of admissions officers, secretaries, office space, public relations and other expenses, might be $50,000.

Evaluation of Students' Educational Histories and Current Status. This task could range from the familiar evaluation of credits earned in formal higher education to the extraordinarily complex appraisal of on-the-job training and experience, instruction received in the armed services or Peace Corps, private music lessons, foreign travel, independent reading, and so on. The simplest cases might require no more than one hour of a clerk's time; in the most complex cases, a whole day might be needed for a professional person to administer a battery of tests (some of which would have to be made up *de novo*) and for interviews with faculty members or faculty committees. The cost could range from $1 to $100 or more per student. The average would probably be at least $40 per student, or an annual total of $80,000.

The Contract. The determination of the students' programs as embodied in their individual contracts would require further counseling and evaluation. Professional specialists might be used, but faculty also would necessarily be involved, either as individual advisors or as committees. The time per student might average two hours or $30 including overhead. The total direct cost for two thousand new students a year would be $60,000.

Counseling While Students Are Enrolled. After students were admitted and before presenting themselves for a degree, they would require counseling, partly by correspondence and some in person. Some of their counseling could be done by professional specialists and some by faculty advisors and other faculty. The average per student might be two hours a year at a direct cost of $30 including overhead. For four thousand students, the total would be $120,000.

Development of Special Courses. The institution would presumably operate courses designed especially for external degree students, and costs would be incurred in developing these courses. Some of these might be correspondence courses using printed materials; some might be courses using TV or other mechanical devices. Assuming that fifty such courses were in operation, that ten new ones were developed each year at a cost of $10,000 a course and ten old ones were thoroughly revised each year at a cost of $3,000 a course, the average annual cost of course development might be $130,000. This figure could be much higher or lower depending on the number and character of the courses.

Instruction. The institution would teach external degree students in the following ways: by admitting them to regular resident courses, by allowing them to take special courses designed for external study, by allowing them to take most courses in the curriculum through independent study and examination, and by recognizing learning acquired through work experience, community service, and other sources. (Students would also be permitted and encouraged to take courses from other institutions.) The costs of these various modes of instruction would be widely different, in some cases higher than resident instruction and in other cases negligible. I would guess that the cost per student course enrollment or equivalent, including correspondence, reading papers and exercises, personal conferences, library use, and tests, would be of the order of $100. If enrolled students were taking on the average the equivalent of two courses a year, or a total of eight thousand courses, the cost would be $800,000.

Degree Examinations. If the institution recorded each student's progress by giving credits and grades on courses (or equivalent units of instruction or learning), the degree could be awarded on the basis of credits earned. However, in view of the diverse and informal character of the learning, the institution might wish to require a final comprehensive examination, probably including a major paper or thesis and an oral interview. An educationally sound program would probably incur terminal costs when the student presented himself for the degree. I would guess that these costs would average $100 per student and would total $40,000 a year if four hundred degrees were awarded.

Campus Conferences. The Open University and other external degree programs sponsor short periods of campus residence for their students. Such a feature is clearly desirable. If four thousand students were present on campus for two weeks each year, the cost aside from board and room might be $75,000, counting such factors as faculty time, cultural events, visiting lecturers, and recreation.

Administrative Costs. A program of the kind envisioned would require a dean and a small administrative staff costing perhaps $100,000 a year.

Overhead. What administrative overhead to charge is a question. Many services available to resident students are not available to external students. The requirements for building space would be minimal. I would judge that an overhead allowance of at least 15 percent of direct costs would be appropriate.

These cost estimates, summarized in Table 15, are very rough guesses. They may be wide of the mark for particular items but probably the total reflects the general order of magnitude. If readers question some of these guesses they may, of course, substitute their own. These figures are not intended to provide a basis for institutional planning.

These estimates suggest that the costs directly associated with awarding a degree (evaluation, contract development, degree exams, campus conferences), as distinct from instruction, are substantial. These costs, amounting to about 15 percent of the total, would be absent if students were engaged in external study for its own sake and not to acquire degrees.

Table 15

ESTIMATED ANNUAL COST OF EXTERNAL DEGREE PROGRAM

Student recruitment	$ 50,000
Evaluation of students' educational histories and current status	80,000
Formulation of students' tailormade educational programs, or contracts	60,000
Counseling while students are enrolled	120,000
Development of special courses (designed for external students but available to resident students)	130,000
Instruction	800,000
Degree examinations	40,000
Campus conferences	75,000
Administrative costs	100,000
Overhead (at 15 percent of direct costs)	220,000
Total	$1,675,000

No provision has been made for student aid, for the cost of advancing and perpetuating knowledge (one of the heaviest elements of overhead in the resident instructional program), or for instructional costs that may be shifted to other institutions such as libraries, museums, employers, social service agencies, and other colleges and universities. From the broad social point of view, all these costs should be included. Those planning external degree programs tend to look only at the incremental direct expenses of the sponsoring institution and not at the total social cost. Needless to say, much more careful studies of cost should be made.

For what they are worth, my guesses result in a cost per student (full-time equivalent) of $1,675 and a cost per student course enrollment (or equivalent) of just over $200. One immediately asks: How does the average of $1,675 per full-time equivalent student compare with average costs for conventional instruction? For the whole United States, the average cost per student (full-time equivalent) in public colleges and universities is about $2,127 and in private institutions $2,731.* These averages include graduate and

* These figures are computed by dividing projected expenditures for

professional students as well as undergraduate students. Average cost for undergraduate instruction is somewhat less. In many institutions it ranges from $1,200 to $1,800.

The estimated cost of an external degree program ($1,675 per full-time equivalent student) is comparable to that of conventional instruction in state institutions because the model under study includes considerable personal attention to individual students, provides tailor-made programs, makes little use of mass media, and does not get full advantage of handling students in large groups called "classes." The reason for choosing this model is that it represents what a single institution awarding an external degree of high quality might be able to offer *now*. It does not suggest what might be possible if hundreds of thousands of students could be "processed" through standardized programs using TV, computers, uniform tests, and so forth. But the know-how, the hardware, the software, and the acceptance of large-scale operation do not yet exist. To estimate costs for that which is only a distant hope and not a near-term possibility would be interesting but not very useful. I would expect, however, that as institutions begin to offer external degrees, and as experience is gained and materials are developed, the costs would tend to decline gradually. I would not expect high-quality programs ever to dispense with substantial infusions of the personal element and so I would not anticipate dramatic cuts.*

Sources of Support

The potential sources of revenue for an external degree program are the same as those for conventional education—tuitions, public appropriations, philanthropic gifts, and endowment income. Should external degree programs receive the same proportion of

student education in 1971–1972 by full-time equivalent enrollments, according to data provided by the National Center for Educational Statistics, *Projections of Educational Statistics to 1979–80* (Washington: U. S. Government Printing Office, 1971), pp. 29, 102.

* It is noteworthy that President Edward Blousteín of Rutgers and President Robert C. Wood of the University of Massachusetts (both institutions are experimenting with an external degree program) recently joined in asserting that the Open University approach to higher education would not be cheaper and easier than the traditional method (*Phi Delta Kappan*, January 1973, p. 364).

these funds as do conventional programs? In my opinion, external and resident degree programs should be considered as comparable in purpose and quality. Students should be able to move freely from one to the other for part or all of their studies and therefore the financing of the two programs should be similar. But several arguments may be advanced for financing the two programs differently, and these should be considered.

First, some people argue that the two student groups will be quite different in background. On the one hand, it is often assumed that external students will have lower incomes and more limited cultural backgrounds than resident students and that they should be encouraged to embark on their studies through tuitions lower in relation to educational cost than those charged resident students. Others assert that external study is educationally more suitable for bright, affluent students with rich cultural backgrounds than it is for students of limited backgrounds. It is no accident that students of the British Open University are drawn largely from the educated classes. Students of limited background should be encouraged to become resident students and to partake of the personal teaching and counseling, the influence of peers, and the cultural atmosphere of the university. Personally, I hold this second view, and I conclude that the fee structure should not necessarily encourage low-income persons to become external students rather than resident students. On this ground, I suggest that tuition for external study should be at least as high, relative to cost, as that for resident study. Now that campuses are located within easy commuting distance of most of the nation's people, there is much to be said on educational grounds for encouraging campus-based instruction. It should, of course, be available to persons of all ages, on a part-time basis, and at convenient times. External study might then be considered a useful supplemental form of learning but not a primary form. On grounds of sheer efficiency, it is hard to beat the organized resident *class*—in which many students are engaged at the same time in the same program of studies. Tailor-made programs, if they contain genuine personal elements of instruction, counseling, and examinations, are likely to be quite costly no matter what the scale of operation.

Second, one can argue that most external students will be earning income and will not be subjected to the noninstructional expenses of college residence. Moreover, many of them will be part-time students whose education and tuition payments will be spread over many years and will therefore not be onerous in any one year. This line of argument supports the case for relatively high tuitions.

Third, one can argue that, if external studies are offered at too low a tuition, resident students will be encouraged to transfer to the external program and the university will lose income from both tuitions and auxiliary enterprises. This argument is perhaps not valid from a long-range social standpoint, but it may be very persuasive from the short-run institutional point of view. It suggests that tuitions for external programs should not be so low as to induce a wholesale exodus of resident students.

Fourth, one can argue that in the early development of external study, tuitions should be low enough to overcome initial resistance to the new and untried and thus to attract substantial enrollments. Sizeable enrollments would then result in more efficient operation and lower cost per student. This argument is an adaptation of the "infant industry" principle. One's judgment about this argument will be influenced by his opinion of the educational potential of external programs and the effect of scale on costs.

On balance, the case for charging external students lower tuitions than resident students, relative to the cost of instruction, is not a strong one. I conclude that external students should bear as high a proportion of the institutional costs assignable to them as is borne by resident students. I am personally an advocate of low tuitions for resident students, and I would make the same argument for external students. But I do not see that there is much of a case for giving external students relative preference over resident students in the matter of tuitions.

I do think, however, that the "infant industry" argument applies to the expensive types of instruction using TV and other large-scale or mass media. To achieve reasonable cost per student, the number of students must be large; to win large enrollments, fees if any must be low or nonexistent. Another consideration is that broadcast TV is publicly available and no one can be excluded from viewing. So a university cannot collect fees for this type of instruction except at the point of granting credit. To allow noncredit students free access to costly instruction while credit-seeking students are forced to pay would be highly discriminatory. Instruction through the mass media probably must be financed largely by government and only incidentally by tuitions. The same situation prevails when various forms of "life experience" are recognized as part of higher learning. The university cannot charge for this type of learning except at the point of granting credit. It would seem discriminatory to charge only those students who apply for credit when others receive the same learning at no cost. To generalize, a university cannot readily charge for those aspects of learning which are part of the general social environment. To the extent that there are costs in providing such learning, they must be borne by government, employers, or whatever public or private agency may be involved.

The *structure* of fees for external study may have to be quite different from that for resident instruction. As indicated, external study may draw on resources in the society for which the university cannot charge. But external degrees involve a variety of specialized services for which charges can be made, namely, admission, evaluation of past educational histories, counseling, instruction under the sponsorship of the university, short-term campus experiences, comprehensive examinations, and so on. To relate student payments to cost of service and to achieve equity among students, a special structure would be devised to assess fees for the various services rendered rather than to charge only annual tuition or fee per credit hour of instruction.

In my view, financing the institutional costs of the external degree would not differ sharply from funding conventional resident instruction except that instruction through the mass media would require heavier subsidies in the early years, and the fee structure would be related to specific services performed rather than to credit hours of instruction. As to whether tuitions should produce a large or small share of the cost, essentially the same arguments would apply to external degree programs as apply to conventional resident instruction.

Financing Students

The basic objective of financing applies to both external students and residents: to open up opportunity to all qualified persons. Any differences in financing the two groups would arise because of a policy encouraging one kind of study over the other or because of differences in the students' circumstances.

As I indicated earlier in discussing tuitions, the case is not strong for a financial system that encourages students to enter external rather than resident study. The weight of argument, at least for large groups of students, may be on the side of encouraging campus study. Perhaps the financial system should be neutral, and external students should be treated, with respect to student aid, like resident students. Any differences in policy would then be based primarily on the different circumstances of the students involved.

Following this principle, young, full-time, undergraduate external students would be treated in exactly the same way as young, full-time, undergraduate resident students. A student would get the same amount of grants and loans no matter which mode he chose. And this principle would also apply to full-time graduate students. However, many or most external students will be part-time students with full-time jobs and many will be older persons. The present student aid system has been designed primarily for young persons who are full-time students, not for part-time students of any age or for adults, whether full-time or part-time. This general weakness of the student aid system requires not a special adjustment to accommodate external students but a general correction for all students.

The solution requires that full-time and part-time students of any age be eligible for aid. The main problems are in establishing need in programs requiring a means test. Here are some of the questions to be resolved: At what age or under what circumstances is a student emancipated from his parents so that the means test applies to him and not to his parents? For clearly emancipated students, should the means test be applied to the individual or to the family group of which he is a part? For example, is a married woman ever eligible for aid even when her husband is able to bear her educational costs? Is aid ever justified to pay for part-time education of persons who are full-time workers?

The answer to these and other similar questions have never been worked out. Solutions need to be found not only for external students but also for resident students. Essentially we should extend the definition of need to apply to all persons seeking education, not just to young, full-time students.

Conclusions

The external degree and the internal degree should not be thought of as separate educational programs but as integrated and interchangeable programs. Educational standards and objectives would be the same, students in course would be free to choose either program wholly or in part, the financing of institutional costs and student expenses would be comparable. This kind of policy would mean that student choices between the two modes of learning would not be strongly influenced by financial considerations (including tuitions and student aid) except as one form might be substantially less costly for equal quality than the other. It would also mean that the financial problems and issues associated with conventional instruction would apply also to external degree programs with few variations.

External degree programs of quality are likely to be quite costly—at least in the short run—and cannot be absorbed into institutional budgets without adequate funding. Efforts to mount these programs without sufficient financing will inevitably hurt performance in both internal and external programs.

BIBLIOGRAPHY

American Academy of Arts and Sciences. *A First Report: The Assembly on University Goals and Governance.* Cambridge, Mass., 1971.

American Council on Education. *Higher Education and the Adult Student, an A.C.E. Special Report.* Washington, D.C., 1972.

American Library Association. *A Strategy for Public Library Change: Proposed Public Library Goals-Feasibility Study.* Chicago, 1972.

ANDREWS, G. J. *A Status Study of Accreditation in Adult and Continuing Education Programs in Higher Education.* Atlanta: Southern Association of Colleges and Schools, 1973.

ASHBY, E. *Any Person, Any Study.* New York: McGraw-Hill, 1971.

Association for Educational Communications and Technology. *The Field of Educational Technology: A Statement of Definition.* Washington, D.C., 1972.

ASTIN, A. "Undergraduate Achievement and Institutional Excellence." *Science,* 1968, *161,* 661–668.

This bibliography draws extensively, although selectively and not exclusively, on W. A. Mahler, *Non-Traditional Study: A Critical Review of the Literature* (Princeton, N.J.: Educational Testing Service, in preparation).

BASKIN, s. *University Without Walls: First Report.* Yellow Springs, Ohio: Union for Experimenting Colleges and Universities, 1972.

BERCHIN, A. *Toward Increased Efficiency in Community Junior College Courses, An Exploratory Study.* Los Angeles: League for Innovation in the Community College, 1972.

BERG, I. *Education and Jobs: The Great Training Robbery.* New York: Praeger, 1970.

BERVE, N. "Legal Bases for Establishment and Regulation of Private Institutions and Corporations." *Higher Education in the States,* 1972, *3*(4), 65–120.

BLAKELY, R. J., AND LAPPIN, I. M. *New Institutional Arrangements and Organizational Patterns for Continuing Education.* Syracuse: Syracuse University Press, 1969.

BOWEN, H. R., AND DOUGLASS, G. K. *Efficiency in Liberal Education: A Study of Comparative Instructional Costs for Different Ways of Organizing Teaching—Learning in a Liberal Arts College.* New York: McGraw-Hill, 1971.

The California State University and Colleges. *The 1,000 Mile Campus.* Rohnert Park, Calif.: Commission on External Degree Programs, 1972.

Carnegie Commission on Higher Education. *Less Time, More Options: Education Beyond the High School.* New York: McGraw-Hill, 1971a.

Carnegie Commission on Higher Education. *New Students and New Places, Policies for the Future Growth and Development of American Higher Education.* New York: McGraw-Hill, 1971b.

Carnegie Commission on Higher Education. *The Fourth Revolution: Instructional Technology in Higher Education.* New York: McGraw-Hill, 1972a.

Carnegie Commission on Higher Education. *The More Effective Use of Resources: An Imperative for Higher Education.* New York: McGraw-Hill, 1972b.

Carnegie Commission on Higher Education. *Reform on the Campus: Changing Students, Changing Academic Programs.* New York: McGraw-Hill, 1972c.

CARP, A., PETERSON, R. E., AND ROELFS, P. *Learning Interests and Experiences of Adult Americans.* Princeton, N.J.: Educational Testing Service. In preparation.

CARROLL, J. "A Model of School Learning." *Teachers College Record*, 1965, *64*, 723–733.

College Entrance Examination Board. CLEP *General Examinations and Subject Examinations: Descriptions and Sample Questions*. New York, 1973.

Commission on Academic Affairs, American Council on Education. "Twelve Issues in Non-Traditional Study." Washington, D.C., 1972. Multilithed.

Commission on Instructional Technology. *To Improve Learning: A Report to the President and Congress of the United States*. Washington, D.C.: U.S. Government Printing Office, 1970.

Commission on Non-Traditional Study. "New Dimensions for the Learner—A First Look at the Prospects for Non-Traditional Study." New York, 1971. (May be obtained from Educational Testing Service, Princeton, N.J., 08540.)

Commission of Postsecondary Education in Ontario. *Draft Report*. Toronto: Ontario Government Bookstore, 1972.

Connecticut Commission for Higher Education. *External Degrees and College Credit by Examinations: Interim Report*. Hartford, 1972.

COYNE, J. AND HEBERT, T. *This Way Out: A Guide to Alternatives to Traditional College Education in the United States, Europe and the Third World*. New York: Dutton, 1972.

CROSS, K. P. *Beyond the Open Door: New Students to Higher Education*. San Francisco: Jossey-Bass, 1971.

CROSS, K. P., AND JONES, J. Q. "Problems of Access." In S. B. Gould and K. P. Cross (Eds.), *Explorations in Non-Traditional Study*. San Francisco: Jossey-Bass, 1972.

DE LISLE, F. H. *Supplement to the March 1972 Compilation of Preliminary Material on Non-Traditional Approaches to Undergraduate Education*. East Lansing: Michigan State University, Office of Institutional Research, 1972.

DICKEY, F. G., AND MILLER, J. W. *A Current Perspective on Accreditation*. Washington, D.C.: American Association for Higher Education, 1972.

DRESSEL, P. L. (Ed.) *The New Colleges: Toward an Appraisal*. Iowa City: American College Testing Program, 1971.

DUNHAM, E. A. *Colleges of the Forgotten Americans*. New York: McGraw-Hill, 1969.

Educational Testing Service. *Proceedings of the Conferences on Career Education.* Princeton, N.J., 1972.

Empire State College. *Bulletin.* Saratoga Springs, N.Y., 1972.

ERIC Clearinghouse on Higher Education. *Bibliography on Aspects of Non-Traditional Study in Higher Education.* Washington, D.C.: George Washington University, 1972.

EURICH, N., AND SCHWENKMEYER, B. *Great Britain's Open University: First Chance, Second Chance, or Last Chance?* New York: Academy for Educational Development, 1971.

FAGIN, M. C. "CLEP Credit Encourages Adults to Seek Degrees." *College Board Review,* Fall 1971, 18–22.

FARMER, M. L. (Ed.) *Counseling Services for Adults in Higher Education.* Metuchen, N.J.: Scarecrow Press, 1971.

Federation of Regional Accrediting Commissions of Higher Education. *A Report on Institutional Accreditation in Higher Education.* Chicago, 1970.

FEINSOT, A. *Breaking the Institutional Mold: Implications of Alternative Systems for Post-Secondary/Higher Education.* White Plains, N.Y.: Knowledge Industry Publications, 1972.

FELDMAN, K. A., AND NEWCOMB, T. M. *The Impact of College on Students.* San Francisco: Jossey-Bass, 1969.

FISCHER, F. B. "Uneasiness in an Era of Romance." *The Spectator,* 1972, *36,* 6.

Five Articles on Non-Traditional Educational Concepts. New York: College Entrance Examination Board, 1972. (Reprinted from *College Board Review,* Fall 1972.)

FLETCHER, M. A. *The Open University, the External Degrees, and Non-Traditional Study: A Selected Annotated Bibliography.* Bryn Mawr, Pa.: American College of Life Underwriters, 1972.

FLEXNER, A. *An Autobiography.* New York: Simon and Schuster, 1960.

GARDNER, J. W. *The Pursuit of Excellence: Education and the Future of America.* New York: Doubleday, 1958.

GLASER, R. "Individuals and Learning: The New Aptitudes." *Educational Researcher,* 1972, *1,* 6.

GOULD, S. B. "New Era for the Public Library." *ALA Bulletin,* 1966, *60,* 585–590.

GOULD, S. B. *Today's Academic Condition.* New York: McGraw-Hill, 1970.

GOULD, S. B., AND CROSS, K. P. (Eds.) *Explorations in Non-Traditional Study.* San Francisco: Jossey-Bass, 1972.

HARCLEROAD, F. F., AND ARMSTRONG, R. J. *New Dimensions of Continuing Studies Programs in the Massachusetts State College System.* Iowa City: American College Testing Program, 1972.

HARLACHER, E. L. *The Community Dimensions of the Community College.* Englewood Cliffs, N.J.: Prentice-Hall, 1969.

HEFFERLIN, JB L. *Cut-Rate Credits and Discount Degrees: Quality Controls of Non-Traditional Study Through State Regulation and Voluntary Accreditation.* Princeton, N.J.: Educational Testing Service. In preparation.

HOLTZMAN, W. H. (Ed.) *Computer-Assisted Instruction, Testing and Guidance.* New York: Harper & Row, 1970.

HOULE, C. O. *The Design of Education.* San Francisco: Jossey-Bass, 1972.

HOULE, C. O. *The External Degree.* San Francisco: Jossey-Bass, 1973.

Innovations in Undergraduate Education: Institutional Profiles and Thoughts About Experimentalism. Report of conference co-sponsored by the New College of the University of Alabama and the National Science Foundation. University, Ala.: New College, 1972.

International Commission on the Development of Education. *Learning to Be.* New York: Unipub, 1972.

JOHNSON, L. B. *Islands of Innovation Expanding: Changes in the Community College.* Beverly Hills, Calif.: Glencoe, 1969.

JOHNSTONE, J. W. C., AND RIVERA, R. J. *Volunteers for Learning: A Study of the Educational Pursuits.* Chicago: Aldine, 1965.

KNIGHT, D. M., AND NOURSE, E. S. (Eds.) *Libraries at Large: Tradition, Innovation and the National Interest.* New York: Bowker, 1969.

KNOWLES, A. S., AND ASSOCIATES. *Handbook of Cooperative Education.* San Francisco: Jossey-Bass, 1971.

KNOWLES, M. S. *The Modern Practice of Adult Education: Andragogy versus Pedagogy.* New York: Association Press, 1970.

LEE, R. E. *Continuing Education for Adults Through the American Public Library.* Chicago: American Library Association, 1966.

LEVIEN, R. E. *The Emerging Technology: Instructional Uses of the Computer in Higher Education.* New York: McGraw-Hill, 1972.

MACLURE, S. "England's Open University." *Change,* 1971, *3,* 62–66.

MADSEN, D. *The National University: Enduring Dream of the U.S.A.* Detroit: Wayne State University Press, 1966.

MAHLER, W. A. *Non-Traditional Study: A Critical Review of the*

Literature. Princeton, N.J.: Educational Testing Service. In preparation.

MARIEN, M. *Beyond the Carnegie Commission: Space-Free/Time-Free and Credit-Free Higher Education.* Syracuse: Educational Policy Research Center, Syracuse University Research Corporation, 1972.

MATHIESON, D. E. *Correspondence Study: A Summary Review of the Research and Development Literature.* Syracuse: ERIC Clearinghouse on Adult Education, 1971.

MC ALLEN ASSOCIATES, LTD. *The Future of Video Cassettes.* London, 1971.

MAC KENZIE, O., CHRISTENSEN, E. L., AND RIGBY, P. H. *Correspondence Instruction in the United States.* New York: McGraw-Hill, 1968.

MELONI, A. *Transfer of College Credits and Off-Campus Learning.* Philadelphia: U.S. Association of Evening College Students, St. Joseph's College, 1972.

Minnesota Metropolitan State College. *MMSC News.* St. Paul, 1972.

National Academy of Engineering, Instructional Technology Committee. *Educational Technology and Higher Education: The Promise and Limitations of ITV and CAI.* Washington, 1969.

National Advisory Council on Extension and Continuing Education *A Question of Stewardship: A Study of the Federal Role in Higher Continuing Education.* Washington, 1972.

National Center for Educational Research and Development, U.S. Office of Education. *New Thrust in Vocational Education.* Washington: U.S. Government Printing Office, 1971.

NEWMAN, F. *Report on Higher Education.* Washington: U.S. Government Printing Office, 1971.

NEWMAN, F. "A Preview of the Second Newman Report." *Change,* May 1972, 28–34.

NEWMAN, J. H. *The Idea of a University.* Discourse VI.

Newsletter of the Commission on Accreditation of Service Experiences. No. 32. Washington, D.C.: American Council on Education, 1969.

Organization for Economic Cooperation and Development, Center for Educational Research and Innovation. *Equal Educational Opportunity.* Paris, 1969.

PERKINS, J. A. (Ed.) *Higher Education: From Autonomy to Systems.* New York: International Council for Educational Development, 1972.

PIFER, A. "Is It Time for an External Degree?" *College Board Review*, 1970–1971, *78*, 5–10.

Policy Institute of Syracuse University Research Corporation. *Newsletter: External Degree Programs*. Syracuse, 1971, 1972a.

Policy Institute of Syracuse University Research Corporation. *Memo from Syracuse*. Adult and Continuing Education, No. 1. Syracuse, 1972b.

PUFFER, C. E., STEFFENS, H. W., LOMBARDI, J., AND PFNISTER, A. O. *Regional Accreditation of Institutions of Higher Education: A Study Prepared for the Federation of Regional Accrediting Commissions of Higher Education*. Chicago: The Federation, 1970. Duplicated.

REICH, D. L. "A Public Library Becomes a CLEP Learning Center," *College Board Review*, 1971, *81*, 29–31.

REID, R. H. *American Degree Mills: A Study of Their Operations and of Existing and Potential Ways to Control Them*. Washington, D.C.: American Council on Education, 1959.

RUDOLPH, F. *The American College and University*. New York: Knopf, 1962.

RUYLE, J., GEISELMAN, L. A., AND HEFFERLIN, JB L. *Non-Traditional Education Opportunities and Programs in Traditional Colleges and Universities, 1972*. Princeton, N.J.: Educational Testing Service. In preparation.

RUYLE, J., HEFFERLIN, JB L., GEISELMAN, L. A., AND KIRTON, A. *Non-Traditional Programs and Opportunities in American Colleges and Universities, 1972*. Princeton, N.J.: Educational Testing Service. In preparation.

SELDEN, W. K. *Accreditation: A Struggle over Standards in Higher Education*. New York: Harper, 1960.

SHARON, A. T. *College Credit for Off-Campus Study*. Report No. 8. Washington, D.C.: ERIC Clearinghouse on Higher Education, 1971.

Sloan Commission on Cable Communications. *On the Cable: The Television of Abundance*. New York: McGraw-Hill, 1971.

SMITH, G. K. (Ed.) *New Teaching, New Learning: Current Issues in Higher Education 1971*. San Francisco: Jossey-Bass, 1971.

SMITH, R. M., AKER, G. F., AND KIDD, J. R. (Eds.) *Handbook of Adult Education*. Washington, D.C.: Adult Education Association of the U.S.A., 1972.

SPURR, S. H. *Academic Degree Structures: Innovative Approaches,*

Principles of Reform in Degree Structures in the United States. New York: McGraw-Hill, 1970.

STRINER, H. E. *Continuing Education as a National Capital Investment.* Washington, D.C.: W. E. Upjohn, Institute for Employment Research, 1972.

Study Commission on Accreditation of Selected Health Educational Programs. "Commission Report." Washington, D.C.: National Commission on Accrediting, 1972.

SUPER, D. E. *Computer-Assisted Counseling.* New York: Teachers College, Columbia University, 1970.

Thomas A. Edison College. *College Proficiency Examination Program.* Trenton, N.J., 1972.

THOMSON, F. C. (Ed.) *The New York Times Guide to Continuing Education in America.* Prepared by the College Entrance Examination Board. New York: Quadrangle Books, 1972.

TROUTT, R. *Special Degree Programs for Adults: Exploring Non-Traditional Degree Programs in Higher Education.* Iowa City: American College Testing Program, 1971.

TURNER, C. P. (Ed.) *A Guide to the Evaluation of Educational Experiences in the Armed Services: Formal Service School Courses, Credit and Advanced Standing by Examination.* Washington, D.C.: American Council on Education, 1968.

United Church of Christ, Office of Communication. *A Short Course in Cable.* New York, 1972.

University of California, Office of the President. *Degree Programs for the Part-Time Student: A Proposal (A Report of the President's Task Force on the Extended University).* Berkeley, 1971.

The University of the State of New York. *The Regents External Degree: Handbook of Information for Candidates.* Albany, 1972.

VALLEY, J. R. *Increasing the Options: Recent Developments in College and University Degree Programs.* Princeton, N.J.: Office of New Degree Programs, Educational Testing Service, 1972.

VERMILYE, D. W. (Ed.) *The Expanded Campus: Current Issues in Higher Education 1972.* San Francisco: Jossey-Bass, 1972.

WALKUP, B. S. *"External Study for Post-Secondary Students: Original and Supplement."* New York: Office of New Degree Programs, College Entrance Examination Board, 1972. Multilithed.

WALTON, W. W. *New Paths for Adult Learning: Systems for Delivery of Instruction in Non-Traditional Programs of Study.* Princeton, N.J.: Educational Testing Service. In preparation.

WARREN, J. R. *Credit and Measurement in Non-Traditional Study.*
    Princeton, N.J.: Educational Testing Service. In preparation.
WILLIAMS, R. L. "Legal Bases for Establishment of Private Institutions
    of Higher Education." *North Central Association Quarterly,*
    1970, *44*(3), 291–298.

INDEX